Who knows what events await us in the new century—both for good and for evil? That's why I believe that the greatest challenge of the next century will not be technological, economic, social, or political. The greatest challenge, instead, will be spiritual, for unless we tame the human heart, the twenty-first century could become the most destructive and cataclysmic in human history.

❧

Billy Graham
Grand Rapids, Michigan, 1999

THE
VOICE
OF THE
HEART

A CALL TO **FULL LIVING**

THE SECOND EDITION

CR

CHIP DODD

All Scripture quotations, unless otherwise indicated, are taken from the HOLY BIBLE, NEW INTERNATIONAL VERSION®. NIV®. Copyright © 1973, 1978, 1984 by International Bible Society. Used by permission of Zondervan Publishing House. All rights reserved.

Scripture quotations marked "NRSV" are taken from the New Revised Standard Version Bible, copyright © 1989, Division of Christian Education of the National Council of Churches of Christ in the United States of America. Used by permission. All rights reserved.

Scripture quotations marked "NKJV" are taken from the New King James Version, copyright © 1982 by Thomas Nelson, Inc. Used by permission. All rights reserved.

Library of Congress Control Number: 2014918238

ISBN: 978-0-9843991-6-1

Spiritual Root System™, The Eight Feelings™, and The Gift of Feelings Chart™ are trademarked by Sage Hill, LLC.

Printed in the United States of America.

Cover design by Lindsey Thompson.

SAGE HILL RESOURCES

www.sagehillresources.com

To Sonya

CONTENTS

☙

The Second Edition
PREFACE

℘

T he publication of the *The Voice of the Heart* occurred with little fanfare in August of 2001. It still remains a quiet book, personal to the reader's life. Amazingly, the book has made its way into hundreds and thousands of lives, directly and indirectly, all around the world.

The first edition is being read and used in places I never envisioned—but hoped for deeply. *The Voice of the Heart* has reached leaders who are looking for the passion in their purpose, groups of pastors who have found refreshment in its simple truths, treatment and counseling professionals who use it to bring the people they wish to help to awareness and freedom of heart, and even a seminary that has called itself to a return to heart. The truths of the book have been used in Sunday School classes, workplace environments, core curriculum in an elementary school, family discussions around the table, between marital partners, during times of solitude of individuals from all walks of life, and by parents who wish to speak to their children's hearts.

The book has a broad audience called humanity, and speaks to those who look to rediscover the doorway into how their hearts were created. My intent in writing *The Voice of the Heart* has always been to help others be who they are made to be, so they can do what they are made to do. The book's material does not change you; only God can change you, but it aids us in becoming more present so we can experience deep change.

Not much has been altered with this second edition of the book. There are some cosmetic changes; a new cover and page layout, along with some minor editorial additions including explanations and clarifications. Most notable is the addition of a "formula" for the gift of feelings (pg. 156). I have used this formula for years when teaching The Eight Feelings™ and have found it consistently effective.

The publication of this edition coincides with a companion Bible study that serves as a resource to help you listen to the voice of your heart. The study shows how feelings fit into the Christian life, and how feelings can bring us closer to the God who desires intimacy with us.

THE EIGHT FEELINGS™

For centuries, people have recognized that if your heart is seen, known, invested, offered and given, then you are considered to be "all in" or "authentic." This authentic experience of the heart allows us to answer the first question God asked mankind: "Where are you?" (Genesis 3:9) It's a question He continues asking us to this day. By knowing our hearts, we see and know where we are and where we need to go.

Feelings, as described in this book, are the first and most important root of the Spiritual Root System™. They help us name what we are experiencing in our hearts. Feelings bring us to the confession of how wonderfully frightening it is to live the mystery of being with God and others.

Feelings, ultimately, are tools we have been given to live fully in a tragic place, where wonder and tragedy, great loves and great losses, intermingle. Our lives cannot yield fully to the eternity we envision in this finite place. But feeling our feelings allow us to "keep heart" in the struggle of living fully, loving deeply, and leading well a life worth living for ourselves and with others.

Over the years, I have been asked multiple times, "How come there are only eight feelings?" Plainly answered: I don't know. Perhaps only eight core feelings are all we need. You must test this for yourself. Let your own exploration of your heart be the answer.

I do believe that every human experience and expression related to feelings can be brought to core emotional experiences. There is a "bottom line" from which one can go no further, and we must name that experience or nothing will happen. Sad is sad no matter how many other ways we say it. All humans know the experience of sadness and its face is shared across all cultures and throughout the history of civilization. The same goes for lonely, hurt, anger, fear, shame, guilt, and glad.

These eight core feelings are the beginning of the expression of all human emotional experience. From these core feelings we can expand the expression to name conditions of the heart such as awe, grief, envy, anxiousness, depression, revenge, delight, and boredom.

It's helpful to understand the feelings as being similar to the three primary colors: red, yellow and blue. These are the only three we have found thus far, and so far the three primary colors have been an amazing gift to allow us to express the astounding magnificence and subtleties of life. Out of the primary colors we have an almost unlimited capacity to mix and make tones and shades that can run into infinity. It's truly wonderful to think about. All the expressions of color start with three primary presentations for us to use, but all true painters need to be fluent in the primary colors.

The feelings don't limit us as much as they allow us to become aware of the potential music of our lives, our own symphony, so to speak.

We can also think of the core feelings as being like musical notes, each core sound being distinct and unto itself. They are limited to a certain range for us to hear them, use them, and create through them. To this day, the most amazing thing is that seven notes in a scale (A, B, C, D, E, F, G) have not limited us with a need to repeat a symphony. They are still being written and conducted without a single repetition. The limits of musical notes in the work of a conductor can leave that person with lifetimes of possibilities. The feelings don't limit us as much as they allow us to become aware of the potential music of our lives, our own symphony, so to speak.

Painters and musicians must accept the primary colors or notes in a scale in order to create. So why are people hesitant to accept the existence of core, foundational feelings that make up the essential design of the human heart? I believe that the struggle is threefold.

First, we fear being confined by limited emotional expression until we realize that the core feelings are only the tools of an artistic and symphonic life experience. We use the primary feelings as a way to build a more artistic and expressive life in which we experience being more present, care more deeply, and express who we are specifically and uniquely more clearly. They allow us to be seen, heard, and known, and to see, listen, and know.

Second, we have been taught to associate feelings with moral judgment against ourselves and others, rather than recognizing true feelings as created within us to allow us to face our selves. Then we can decide what we need to do with these feelings to live truthfully and behave morally. We have been taught to think of feelings as bad because of the number of people who hide their true feelings and do damage to others to avoid the vulnerability of the truth.

Feelings are not impulses that need to be controlled; they are tools that we need to learn how to use well so that we do not behave impulsively and act out without the ability to take responsibility. They are tools that allow us to live truthfully and move responsibly. They are good because they allow us to process life experience—not as a mechanical rationale of moving ourselves about like widgets, but to process life as a living, breathing experience over which we really do not have control. Feelings are required material to be able to live the human experience rather than a mechanistic objectification of our existence.

Third, feelings are good, just like organs of the body are good. They are simply a part of us, designed a certain way to do certain functions so that the living, emotional and spiritual organism can have full functioning, i.e., live fully in relationship. Your lungs are good, as is your bladder, spleen and so on. The healthier they are, the more able the organism is to live out the full capability of one's purposes. The organ that malfunctions will signal that, "something is awry" so that help may arrive to return to the good of functioning. The organs of your body are not moral, but they are good. I think many people have been taught, sadly, that feelings themselves are wrong, when it's the actions of being irresponsible with these feelings that cause so much harm—even when a person appears to be acting honorably while being in denial about their internal emotional experience.

As I close this preface, I wish to say how sorry I am that while the feelings themselves aren't negative, much of life is. So much of life is about sorrow and fear and injustice and disruption and beauty achieved momentarily and then wonder collapsing. We live with memories unfinished and longings incomplete, so much so that God blessed us with tools that bring us to a life lived fully amidst the tragedy and wonder of life.

The feelings are good; they move us to the gifts that they are made to bring us in the hands of the artists who use them—the tools of the trade of living fully. The gifts allow us to have life, love, and legacy in a tragic place. I'm sorry that we need all the tools, even though I cherish their results. I still wish we only needed the one you most think you want—gladness.

But until then, I pray that you will take on the passion of living a life that will bring you to gratitude. Gratitude in a world in which your dreams will always be greater than the life you will have. I am grateful that God has given us the ability to feel because of the gifts they can initiate. I am also glad that this book holds steady in the words I still find fresh and deep; in the seventeen years since writing the book, it still remains true and exciting.

THE
VOICE
OF THE
HEART

I pray also that the eyes of your
heart may be enlightened in order
that you may know the hope to
which he has called you.

—Ephesians 1:18 NIV

INTRODUCTION

☞

The first time I saw David I was speaking to a group of patients at a treatment center in a suburban Dallas hospital. I noticed David when he came through the lecture room for a little while, stood for a couple of minutes, and then left.

Looking at him, I felt deep sadness because it was obvious that he had gone beyond his own ability to endure. The expression on his face looked like sheer pain plastered into a smile.

I didn't see him again until three weeks later when I got a phone call from a psychiatric nurse requesting that I begin seeing David as an individual patient.

It turned out that between the lecture and the phone call, David had been allowed to go home from the inpatient site on a temporary leave. Once at home, David fed his horses; then, in desperation and numbness over his marriage, his internal pain, and his life, he hanged himself in his barn.

Seconds later, David's wife came out to the barn and found him hanging. She shoved him out of the noose and called the paramedics. David was already dead. When the

EMTs arrived, they resuscitated him and rushed him to a nearby hospital.

His wife came into the hospital waving a living will, saying, "No life-support systems!" David's parents arrived about the same time, and after some heated discussion between the doctors, his wife, and his parents, David was moved to the intensive care unit and put on life support.

When he was barely physically able, David's parents transferred him from the hospital with doctors' permission and took him back to the treatment center's inpatient unit. That is where I first met David face-to-face.

A nurse who was familiar with my work and beliefs recommended that I see him. She hoped that I could help in what seemed like a hopeless situation.

David was lying in his bed, motionless, with the same frozen smile on his face. The room was dark except for sunlight spilling through slits in the half-closed blinds. David was still fragile after being transferred from the intensive care unit. When he breathed, he groaned with physical and emotional pain—the pain of a wounded body and a broken heart.

I quietly sat down beside him. Fearful, I wondered to God what I was doing there. After some time, I told him my name. Then I said, "David, you've hit bottom. As it turns out, when you hit, you fell through a skylight and kept dropping."

Beside me lay a man who had cried so deeply that he had no more tears. All he could do was lie there and groan between breaths. I remember telling him, "There is no farther to fall; you're in the bottom of the pit."

I promised him that there was a ladder that reached

from where he lay in the darkness all the way back to the surface of life. I told him that when he was ready to take a step, I would take a step. When he was ready to walk, I would walk. When he was ready to run, I would run.

I also told him that any time he needed to come back to the bottom of the pit and sit in hopelessness or rest in grief, that I would watch over him. Most important, I promised him that he would quit before I would quit because I wasn't going to quit.

Through a long process, David moved from being bedridden to sitting up, to using a wheelchair, to limping down the hall, then to walking freely.

Although David's wounded body was healing, his heart remained broken. His shame, despair, and hopelessness continued to drive him toward death as the solution to his pain. In time, these experiences slowly translated into grief, loneliness, anger, and a healthy hunger for the pain to end.

David walked through great emotional and spiritual pain. We worked exclusively through the issues of the heart, the storehouse of the self. Probably most painful for him was his dare to hope again with his heart's desires and longings, to need again, and to feel again. In using his heart, David courageously climbed back to the surface of life.

David's parents were involved in the process, as was one of his old childhood friends. They came to the hospital as often as they could, and David and his family grew closer than they had ever been.

About a year after our work began, and months after leaving the hospital, David returned to his old job as an excavator. Within a few months, he lost his father to a massive coronary. Fortunately, each man had spoken many words of love and truth to the other before his father's death. David had chosen to live fully from his heart before his father died and he still does so.

Today, I get an occasional card from David. Not only has he resumed his work, but he also returns to the hospital from time to time to share the story of his recovery from death to life, from resignation to acceptance, and from apathy to love.

QUESTIONS OF THE HEART

Although this small piece of David's story is an extreme example of brokenness, it has a lot in common with you and me. David did not know his heart. For David, like many of us, it took a crisis to expose his heart's muted voice. But from deep within him rose the same nagging questions that we all ask ourselves late at night when silence settles about us.

- What's the point?
- Is there more?
- Will I ever be loved?
- How much longer can I do this?
- Is God really here?
- Is God good?

These troubling questions of our hearts do not go away. No matter what we do to silence them, our hearts will not be stilled. They demand to be answered before we can live a truly fulfilled life.

Answers are not always easily found and are rarely painless when we learn them. But by avoiding these issues, we rob ourselves of the heart's true potential for joy. Instead of facing truth, we seek counterfeit solutions, trying to avoid the neediness and vulnerability so often found with the truth.

We drink to excess. We seek pharmaceutical solutions to avoid emotional problems. We pursue status, power, and achievement. We use religion and ego-centered spirituality as a drug. We pray for God to stay away so that we can hide from the truth. We furiously erect walls around our hearts. We actively pursue behaviors that we believe will silence our hearts without listening to our hearts' calls for gratification. We leave our hearts unexplored, and they become corrupted by the very things we do to satisfy them.

The counterfeit solutions that we manufacture for the heart's questions do not truly feed the heart's hunger. The questions simply come back louder than before, and we are eventually left wondering if there even are answers.

Answers do indeed exist, and they move us into a life much bigger than we have ever dared to imagine. The answers we find show us that life is about living fully. We learn that life is not simply about being happy or satiated. It's about living fully in intimate relationship with ourselves, with others, and with God, which is a joy unto itself (even in pain). Therein, we become gratified. To find the answers, we need to know where to look.

Like David, we all have pits of struggle, despair, and pain to climb out of. We have questions that need answers and lives that need to be fully lived.

Unless you can face this truth, you probably need to

stop reading now—for you this book will be meaningless.

This book is an invitation to rediscovery. It helps you find what you lost and reawaken what is asleep. It will hopefully be a tool to help you knock down the walls around your heart.

Throughout the book you will find pages that illuminate many of the impaired and healthy states of living. These terms are denoted by illustrations of impaired and full-living trees respectively.

This book calls you to begin a journey home that starts with listening to your heart and understanding how you were made.

I have been using the Spiritual Root System™ for over 20 years as a genuine way to reintroduce people to their hearts, and in turn to full lives that can be intimately shared with others and with God.

The Spiritual Root System™ has been deeply informed by my formal education, but more importantly its origin grew out of my own recovery of heart and was created in the crucible of relationship with hundreds of people I have been privileged to work with.

For many of us on this journey, things that seem impossible become possible, damaged relationships are repaired, and a pursuing God starts to make sense in a real and good way.

The path is hard climbing at times, but I found the walk worth every step. I pray that you will, too.

I do not understand what I do.
For what I want to do I do not do,
but what I hate I do.

—Romans 7:15

CHAPTER 1

The
SPIRITUAL ROOT SYSTEM

ᘓᗜ

God created you and me as emotional and spiritual creatures—created to live fully in relationship with ourselves, with others, and with God. We are image bearers of God, actually stamped in our hearts with a hunger to live fully. However, this hunger cannot be gratified unless we are emotionally and spiritually nourished by relationships.

When you and I live out of our heart-stamped characteristics, we discover our need for relationship. Without a doubt, we are relational beings. Even in utero, relationship occurs. There's a response from the child to the mother's voice, to the father's voice. There's a response to music. The child in the womb recoils from yelling voices.

When the child is born into life, the baby immediately starts to respond to how he or she was made—to a knowledge that cannot be verbally or cognitively articulated. It can only be lived from the heart.

THE BEGINNING OF THE JOURNEY

Long before you developed a cognitive or verbal capacity, you responded to life with other knowledge—your feelings. As a baby, your feelings moved you into living fully in relationship.

As soon as you left the womb, you reached out with a grasping reflex for the comfort and closeness of a caregiver. You cried out with heart for your needs to be addressed. You nursed, attempting to bring life and relationship into yourself. You were, of course, reacting biologically. However, you were also responding emotionally and spiritually.

...the heart's capacity for emotional expression and spiritual relationship can be greater than our own biological instincts.

This initial relational movement began your journey as the only creature that is capable of transcending its biology. Astoundingly, the heart's capacity for emotional expression and spiritual relationship can be greater than our own biological instincts.

I remember being in the delivery room when each of my two sons was born. At that moment I made a thousand passionate promises about what I would do: how I would protect him, how I would take care of him, how no harm would come to him, how I would always be there.

"You'll never be harmed. Your heart will never be broken. No matter what happens, you will be safe." The instant I made those promises, they were already broken because they were impossible to keep.

Nevertheless, all this love, all this hope, all this tremendous recognition of my son's worth, I offered freely out of my heart without expecting anything in return.

I offered this love to a creature who by the world's

standards of productivity and performance had little value. I was promising all these things to a blue-footed, banana-headed alien who could do nothing, give nothing, and offer nothing except his feelings and needs. And yet, I knew in my heart that he possessed incredible, inescapable, undeniable worth.

We all carry the capacity to recognize value in babies who can't do anything, and we all carry the same capacity to remember that value in ourselves. We can't stop it within us. Our hearts are made like that, regardless of the culture, the abuse, or the religion that has impacted us. However, we can deny and forget our own worth.

So why do we love newborns so unashamedly?

What actually happens is that as we look at infants, our hearts identify their inherent worth and often our own long-forgotten worth. We value that experience of the heart because it is truth. In this open-hearted moment, we recognize the incredible value of this very useless little creature.

A newborn can eat, sleep, cry, feel, need, long, desire, and hope. That's all she can do. She is an emotional and spiritual creature who is made to live fully in relationship.

Primary to existence, this child needs emotional and spiritual food. If provided that nourishment, she will maintain a sense of worth and expand self-love into love beyond herself.

I can provide my children with all of the great external riches—material, academic, experiential—yet if they are not rich emotionally and spiritually, I will have children who do not see themselves for who they are made to be. They will lack an understanding about why they were born (to live fully) and how they were created (in the image of God).

If we are taught to deny or forget our emotional and

spiritual makeup, we travel farther and farther and farther away from the truth of the maternity ward and from our own sense of worth.

We end up experiencing lives of resignation. We try to make our hearts believe and accept a false reality of not hoping for much. We subordinate ourselves to the lie that our lives don't have great worth except through performance or merit.

We do things because we ought to instead of awakening to the desire within our hearts that hunger for truth and hunger to do things because we passionately desire to do them.

We defend against knowing ourselves and letting others know us, making ourselves alone. We end up living lives of lies, defending against how we really feel, and surviving in desperation. We wind up so far from that maternity ward that we can't even recognize how we are truly made. We live far below the heights for which we were made.

But if you risk acknowledging and understanding the substance of your heart, you begin to see your life change and grow and become full.

You no longer live in resignation. You find acceptance.
You no longer practice hopelessness. You live in hope.

You no longer live in demand. You live in expectation.
You no longer live in lust. You live in passion.

You no longer manage. You have faith in mystery.
You are no longer helpless. You recognize your powerlessness.

You are no longer defensive. You establish a healthy identity.
You no longer live in worry. You live in faith.

You no longer live in judgment. You live in discernment.
You no longer live in pride. You live in confession.

You no longer justify yourself. You seek forgiveness.
You no longer live in penance. You hunger to change.

You no longer survive. You have full life.

In the journey of life there are two roads. One road, well traveled as it is, keeps us in the existence of survival—never fully knowing ourselves, never fully knowing others, and never fully finding the abundant life for which we were searching anyway. We spend our existence toiling to make life happen, and all it gets us is a grave, a marker, and a date.

The other leads to full life—a road along the heights that is rough going, yet joyous and full. This is the way of the heart. On this road our hearts become clarified, freed, and made new.

Once we decide to leave the road of survival and travel on the path of full life, we need to journey back to our hearts and begin again. We need to acknowledge that the very nature of life proves that we need to be reborn so the survivor-self can die and the true self can arise.

THE STRUCTURE OF THE HEART

He will be like a tree planted by the water that sends out its roots by the stream. It does not fear when heat comes; its leaves are always green. It has no worries in a year of drought and never fails to bear fruit. —Jeremiah 17:8

Picture your heart and its growth as a system of spiritual and emotional roots that need spiritual and emotional nourishment. Out of sustenance and growth of the root system, you are made aware of and able to pursue abundant living.

This root system is so powerful that, like the old tree on Main Street, it doesn't matter how many sidewalks are put down, sooner or later the roots are going to reach up and snap the sidewalk in two. This is how your heart is made.

Either you deal with your heart, or the attempts to stop your heart's voice will create such conflict that it will break your life into pieces. However, if you deal with your heart, it's guaranteed that when the tough times come, you will be okay.

Healthy Living

The diagram on the right page represents life lived fully out of a maturing heart. The tree planted by the water grows full, rich, and productive with the capacity to attract and genuinely give to others out of its own abundance.

Below the surface are the roots, the structure and substance of the heart. They are our feelings, needs, desires, longings, and hope. If your heart receives the emotional and spiritual nourishment of relationship in all its meaning, then you become who and what you were made to be.

By surrendering to your heart's true expression, you can live abundantly. Your thirsts and hungers will be gratified. Your feelings, needs, desires, longings, and hope will lead you to full life.

Does the full life mean that storms won't come? No, they will. Lightning won't strike? No, it will. Does it mean that disease won't infect the tree and rob it of its physical health? It certainly can.

Ultimately, living fully means more than happiness, comfort, or thrills. You have the capacity to experience true joy, yet you are equally capable of grieving deeply while holding on to hope. Full life means you can expect great things in the midst of great loss. You can accomplish many good things while still needing to be forgiven for the harm that you have caused.

The Spiritual Root System™
A Guide to Full Living

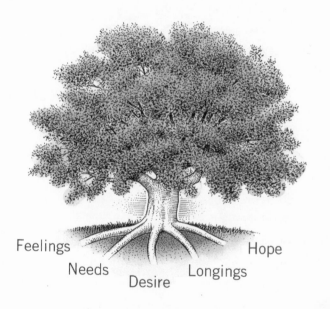

Feelings   Hope

Needs   Longings

Desire

Impaired Living

> I will remove from you your heart of stone
> and give you a heart of flesh. —Ezekiel 36:26

If your heart does not draw deeply from the emotional and spiritual nourishment of relationship, you will suffer and unintentionally grow into a spindly bush that never fully lives. If you grow up in a world where feelings are shamed, needs bastardized, desires thwarted, longings minimized, and hope diminished, then your roots do not receive the nourishment needed for growth. You are taught to ignore or be ashamed of how you are truly made.

Throughout life all of us have received deep emotional and spiritual wounds, often from the people we trust the most. Because of our love and need for these caregivers, we become capable (for survival's sake) of rejecting our hearts and denying our wounds.

We quit drinking deeply from the waters of emotional and spiritual life. We quit trusting the heart's thirst to be known, seen, fed, and expanded. Instead of remaining vulnerable to growth, we resign our hearts to blocking all intrusions of relationship (and, ultimately, love) because of the fear that: (1) relationship is not real, and (2) relationship is real, but it will not last.

However they occur, if we do not address these woundings on an emotional and spiritual level by admitting and surrendering to how our hearts are made, they will never heal. Instead of healing, we try to defend our hearts against further pain, leaving our true pain ignored and unattended.

By rejecting our hearts and denying their contents, we

have become spindly bushes living in resignation, steeped in denial, rationalization, and manipulation.

We may have amassed power, wealth, and knowledge, yet we still feel ashamed of how we are made.

To hide our hearts, we work to acquire defenses so that our hearts can't be touched. We lower our spiritual and emotional expectations. We don't expect much from ourselves. We pretend we don't need much from others. And we deny how much we distrust and need God.

We become experts at practicing hopelessness—not believing that our hearts' yearnings are real, denying that our feelings matter, and lacking the faith that we are really made as persons of immense value. We deny our innate wishes for more life and love.

To protect ourselves from hopelessness, we pretend that things don't matter. We act as if nothing "gets to us." We chant the mantra "Sticks and stones may break my bones, but words will never hurt me," knowing all the time that it is a lie. The harms, both spoken and unspoken—the rejection of our hearts in relationship—break our hearts.

We practice hopelessness by not taking chances with our hearts. To keep our hearts' legitimate hungers silenced (or at least muffled), we feed on counterfeit fulfillments—affairs, power, sex, wealth, religiosity, alcohol, demands on others—so that we can have control. We become so entrenched in this habit of hopelessness—defending against hope that will not be silenced—that some of us even kill ourselves (suicide is an attempt to kill hope, to make the ache for real life stop).

THE FIVE ROOTS

In order to grow from spindly trees into full trees, we need to reawaken to and acknowledge our inborn Spiritual Root System™. The five roots that drink in the nourishment of life are feelings, needs, desire, longings, and hope.

1. Feelings

Feelings speak the language of the heart. We come out of the womb experiencing life through our feelings. They are primary to our human experience and awaken us to our hearts. We use feelings to communicate our God-given hunger for relationship. Unless we rediscover our ability to feel deeply and express feelings clearly, we will never find full life.

2. Needs

I once believed food, clothing, and shelter were all we needed for life. That is far from true.

You and I were created with needs much more powerful than food, clothing, and shelter. We have emotional and spiritual needs that reveal the truth about our vulnerability. We have the need for:

- security
- touch
- significance
- attention
- guidance
- support
- freedom

- safety
- belonging
- grieving
- sexuality
- accomplishment
- nurturing
- trust

An example of the importance of our needs is our need for

attention. Receiving attention means to be tended to, nurtured so that we can grow. Fruit trees produce fruit based upon how well they are tended to. People are much the same way. However, many of us believe that the need for attention ends at adolescence, or that it's just childish dependency.

The truth is that the more mature of heart we are, the more we need to be tended to so that we may give more. The more deeply replenished we are, the more we have to give.

All needs are similar in this way. Unless we take full ownership of our needs, we will use illegitimate ways of meeting legitimate needs. For example, the legitimate need for attention from a spouse can be met illegitimately by another in an affair.

Needs don't change, they are part of our hearts. They will find a way to be met, somehow.

3. Desire

Desire, the hunger for life, is the energy that moves you toward fulfillment and expression. Desires are pure glimpses of who you're made to be. If you are in contact with the depths of your heart, you will desire whatever is noble, pure, lovely, admirable, true, right, and excellent—and you will hunger to participate in creating these things.

However, if you are ashamed of your desires or if you are defended against needing, then your desires will become corrupted and tarnished, and they will lead you to living in hopelessness, apathy, and resignation. For instance:

> Your hunger for beauty becomes a lust for sex;
>
> Your hunger for truth becomes the dogma of control or rigidity;

Your hunger for nobility becomes an arrogant search for causes that feed your ego; and

Your hunger for justice becomes a demand that others be conformed to your will.

As a result of this corruption, you become afraid of pure desires that require vulnerability because of the hurt you have felt when they were rejected or unfulfilled in the past.

Exposing a true desire is a tremendous act of vulnerability because it shows how much we want something. Revealing this much truth renders us naked. Desires show how much we hunger for something bigger than ourselves to fulfill us. Desires are powerful enough—whether corrupt or pure—that we will endure emotional, spiritual, and physical pain to obtain them. The same person who once lusted for drugs may now passionately desire to remain free in recovery from addiction.

Desires show how much we hunger for something bigger than ourselves to fulfill us.

Pure desire differs from impaired expressions of desire. For example, if in my innate desire for excellence I try to protect myself from the vulnerability of failure, I become a perfectionist or overachiever. What I claim to have done in the name of excellence is actually about hiding my vulnerability and fear of failing. Hiding my vulnerability demands that others recognize me for my achievement.

True excellence comes from admitting and learning from mistakes. Fear of vulnerability blocks the desire for excellence because I "cannot" fail.

The desire for true intimacy is admirable. However, if I am ashamed of myself and believe that no one can love me for who I am, then I resort to excitement, performance, or "stuff" as a surrogate for intimacy. I offer those things to myself, others, and God instead of my heart.

4. Longings

Longings are the heart's deep emotional and spiritual cravings for justice, rest, peace, safety, and home. These soulful powers yearn for fulfillment. They are both painful and wonderful—painful because they will never be completely fulfilled on earth, wonderful because we can have enough to teach us that we can wait for more.

When our hearts cry out in the longing for justice, we look around the world and see how far from justice we actually live.

For instance, if you've ever seen a child in a hospital bed with tubes coming out of his body, you've experienced the longing for justice. Looking at the child in that bed, something in you cries "NO!" You don't even have to know the child to recognize your longing for pain and disease to end.

The longing for rest lets us know when a job is complete, yet leaves us with the wish for a time when no more jobs follow. Each of us longs for the day when tasks end and work is over. We long for a soulful rest when we don't *have to* anymore. Even the joy of challenge wears us down. We all long for a rest that will fill us completely.

We long for peace. The longing is an inner craving for tranquility and contentment. Even in the bustle of life, we can have extended periods of serenity. At those same periods, we also recognize that we cannot have enough peace and that the peace we do experience is only temporary—problems don't stop. Yet we still long in our hearts for a place where peace never ends.

We long for safety, an end to pain. Our hearts ache for a shoulder we can put our heads against, arms big enough to reach around us, and a voice that can tell us truthfully, "It's okay now." Each of us also deeply longs for a place called home. It is the eternal in us wishing to return to God.

5. Hope

Hope is the heart's passion for life. It is the inextinguishable flame that illuminates our hunger for relationship. Hope is the voice that calls us to look, to believe, and to trust. To risk hoping builds faith.

When you were born, you reached out and grasped the hand of your caregiver, sucked in life, and cried out to be heard by someone who could still your cry. This behavior expresses hope—the belief and trust—that another will meet you in your reaching out. Hope thwarted leads to despair, yet even despair doesn't stop hope.

No matter what has happened to you in your life, you still have the capacity to reach out in hope to another—whether it is a parent, friend, spouse, or God. Being met by another in your hope creates faith because it provides substance for the previously unseen. New experiences of hope fulfilled build faith.

Hope grants us the willingness and the ability to go on. Hope is the spiritual and emotional energy that makes us get up and turn the next corner to see if the answers might be there.

THE WOUNDINGS OF LIFE

Life is an abandoning process. When we move into life with the spontaneous expression of childhood, the pure hunger for relationship, we get knocked around. We are lied to, put down, teased, and rejected.

If you experienced a childhood where your spiritual and emotional roots were nourished, then you were prepared when life's abandonments came. You knew to listen to your heart so that you could grow through the pain into acceptance and develop greater wisdom through the whole experience. Rather than defend against pain, you used it to grow—and are still growing today.

However, if your childhood thwarted, shut down, minimized, or taught you to deny your roots, then your capacity for growth was diminished, leaving you unprepared for the abandonments of life (or, for that matter, for experiencing the love of God). Instead of growing, you put on layers of protection. Listening to your heart lead only to pain.

Each of us has received woundings, whether we're from a "good" home, or an impaired home. If we find healing and understanding in these woundings through our hearts, they will help us grow and prepare us for what we're made to accomplish.

A person who succeeds at living is capable of experiencing the heart most deeply when life's woundings come, and then getting up and moving on to new heights. In other words, before we climb back on the horse, we must first experience the fall, take account of the loss, and decide when we are ready to get back on.

It is the family's job to help a child (based upon the bent of the child's heart) to develop mature feelings, needs, desires, longings, and hope. Through this maturity the child is prepared to handle more and more of life's pain and complexity, and gain wisdom in the process.

Many of us were raised in ways that taught us to reject, numb, or hide our hearts.

Many of us were raised in ways that taught us to reject, numb, or hide our hearts. We ended up as adults who don't know how to use our feelings in order to live fully. Consequently, we don't know how to handle our woundings except by being more defensive, survival oriented, or self-sufficient. We develop philosophies that excuse our own impairments, and we eventually become wounders ourselves.

Through life's woundings, we have either deepened our ability to use our roots, or we have attempted to squash our capacity to live fully from our hearts. Our desires either grow into something positive, or they wither into the energy we use to defend, depress, and smother our roots.

In an attempt to prevent new wounds, we learn to defend with survival methods. While these methods work, they also block old wounds from healing. Survival methods work because they hide our hearts from relationship with ourselves because we deny our vulnerability, with others because what we present is a facade, and with God because what we are living is in direct conflict with how we are made.

Survivors

Survivors experience and endure pain by defending against the exposure of what's happening in their hearts. Because of deep woundings, they have given up on the truth of their hearts. They resign themselves to pretending that the heart doesn't matter—that feelings, needs, desires, longings, and hope aren't essential for life. Instead of living vulnerably in the light, survivors keep their hearts hidden in the shadows, for "survival's sake."

When genuine opportunity to grieve, resolve, accept, or heal these wounds arises, survivors become:

- opposed to their vulnerability,
- terrified of exposing their hearts,
- deeply ashamed of the truth of their hearts, and
- resigned to believing that they are not "worth the trouble."

If you recognize yourself as a survivor, it's okay. You have reasons to be defended. Your pain is real, as is your history of denying its existence. But if you stay the same, life remains like it has already been for you.

In truth, survival living is war against the heart. Even though we are in survival mode, we still hear the heart crying for life. To protect ourselves, we find things to distract ourselves from its cries.

We binge on multiple distractions so we won't feel lonely.

We drink excessively because we don't believe there is anything better.

We amass power so we won't feel afraid.

We suffer depression to escape from anger.

> We practice quid pro quo as an illusion of intimacy.
>
> We fight for the status quo to keep from facing our fear, or we fight for change to avoid the pain of waiting.
>
> We go to church worshiping the ritual that allows us to safely avoid knowing God.
>
> We do all of these things to avoid relationship with our hearts, others' hearts, and God's heart.

However understandable these justifications used to defend ourselves are, they eventually destroy our hearts. The following statements are a few examples of the destruction we commit against ourselves.

"That's life." This rationalization minimizes the true aches and woundings of life, allowing us to keep going. It keeps us from trusting our hearts' desires for peace, intimacy, and love. We consider ourselves "realists," but actually we have hearts resigned to cynicism. We doubt everything true and good because we are afraid to face how much life really hurts. We need to admit our pain in order to see what our hearts desire. Trying to pretend that something doesn't matter won't make the heart's wish go away. By naming our pain, we discover what we deeply desire in our hearts for life's sake.

"I'm different." This is an effort to escape the same aches and pains we all experience by trying to raise ourselves above human frailty. Its antithesis is "I'm hopeless." (Hopelessness says that instead of raising myself above human frailty, "I'm so worthless that there is no sense in even trying.") But both destructions stop us from experiencing the intimacy for which our hearts hunger. Although we need to recognize our uniqueness, we also need to develop the ability to humbly see how we are like others—susceptible to life's pains and to making mistakes.

"At least I don't . . ." This is a defense to avoid personal responsibility by shaming others' needs for us and love for us. It sounds like, "At least I don't play golf as much as Steven. He's never home. Why are you complaining?" Or, "At least I don't go shopping as often as Heather, she spends all their money on clothes." This type of response belittles the needs of those who want relationship from us by shaming them. It also minimizes our own need to make changes and communicates our unwillingness and fear to be intimate with others.

"Don't sweat the small stuff; it's all small stuff." This rejects the sensitivity of the heart and its ability to value even small things. It also rejects others who need our care. It hides our hearts and pushes others away because we tell them that their pain or concerns are not important. We need to be able to discern different levels of importance without ignoring the heart's voice.

"I can't do that," or **"It's not worth my time."** These keep us from learning because we refuse to risk failure. In order to protect ourselves from exposing our desires, we belittle ourselves ("I can't do that") or we belittle the experience ("It's not worth my time"). Both statements keep us from risking new experiences and shield us from pain. In dictating future outcomes, we miss discovering new gifts.

"That's too much to handle." This excuse avoids depending on another person or on God, which is what we are made to do. The truth is that life is "too much to handle"—alone. We need to know our limits so we can ask for help.

"I would do it for you." This is manipulation to shame someone else into meeting our needs. It always leads to resentment. On the surface it is a way to justify our right to be loved. This is a belief that enslaves us to relationships based on have tos, ought tos, and shoulds. Giving is a gift, not a form of manipulating another's heart.

"I should be grateful." This statement harms us by keeping us from revealing the parts of the heart that we fear will be rejected. It stops us from desiring the abundant life. It demeans our God-made hunger for more. We need to be grateful, but not as a command. It is okay to be sad, lonely, hurting… in pain even when we have many blessings in our lives.

"They don't know what they're talking about." This statement becomes a way to stop us from trusting others by discounting their ideas, opinions, gifts, and abilities. It keeps us from risking relationship. If we don't trust, we will miss opportunities. While not everyone is trustworthy, distrust without discernment is a blanket rejection of everyone.

Self-esteem—Nourishment for Survivors

The tragic secret of survivors is that they don't believe they have great inherent worth. They believe worth comes from performance, production, and the approval of others. As we become more and more survival-oriented, we get farther away from the truth that has been in our hearts from the very beginning—our own worth. We emerge with a sense that our value is based only on our ability to contribute or perform. Ironically, some of us base our worth on our refusal to perform.

Self-esteem is something we manufacture in order to create a sense of control or power.

To avoid facing our low sense of worth, we try to compensate by building self-esteem. Self-esteem is a way to be in control of our image in order to protect our sense of something missing within our hearts. Through self-esteem, achievements are a way of creating hope. Esteem for self rises and falls based upon the grade of our last performance. Sadly, we forget that our value is inherent at birth.

Unfortunately, our culture trumpets the philosophy of self-esteem. Self-esteem is a movement of thought that's based upon creating a sense of confidence through self-ability or self-sufficiency. Self-esteem is something we manufacture in order to create a sense of control or power. It offers a false sense of worth based not on our inborn gifts, but on our achievement only: "I did; therefore I am." This is the opposite of God and what God made us to be: "I am; therefore I do."

We toil away trying to acquire worth that we once knew but discarded when we rejected the truth of our hearts. The tragedy is that anything that can be constructed can be deconstructed. We've insanely been taught that we can create our own worth. We spend our lives forever building our self-esteem, having it destroyed, and building it back up again.

The great "solution" to our lives' problems is to try harder, often finding the next "new" technique that will improve our chances at success. Madison Avenue propagates this culture and helps us numb our lives. We focus on the appetite of our stomachs, not the hungers of our hearts.

By self-esteem's standards, my worth comes from my perception of your evaluation of me, or my evaluation of myself compared to you. We have replaced our innate sense of self-worth with a thing called self-esteem. We are actually made by God to have self-love.

Self-esteem's traps (productivity and performance) cause many survivors to make their offices home. Nowhere are we more exposed than at home, where people see us as we really are. Therefore, as survivors we end up living at our offices to avoid having to face our woundedness at home.

At the office, we attempt to create a place of safety away from home. For survivors, the office can become a place to experience relationship without truly revealing themselves. They hide behind titles, sales goals, to-do lists, and profit margins so that they don't have to be truly known. Without revealing their hearts, they try to establish relationships through intellectual ideas, discussions, and kicking around plans. They confide inappropriately in their co-workers, telling them secrets about themselves, because they don't entrust their hearts to the people they most care about.

The same is true figuratively. Our office is in our head. It's the place where we plan, strategize, count costs, compare ourselves, evaluate others, and consider options before making decisions. Survivors try to make homes at the office—find peace, serenity, fulfillment, and intimacy at work or in their minds.

But in truth, home is where your heart is. We need to go home to the heart before our lives can be full. As survivors, the most difficult journey we may ever take is only 18 inches long, from our head (office) to our heart (home).

DIAGNOSIS: HEART PROBLEM

> As water reflects a face,
> so a man's heart reflects the man.
> —Proverbs 27:19

We are people with heart pains and heart problems which require heart solutions. However, we attempt to solve heart problems with intellect, willpower, and morality, which are no more effective for solving heart problems than a shovel is for cutting a board. Both the shovel and the board are good, but the combination is ineffective. Eventually, I can hack away with a shovel to cut the board, but it's senseless to misuse that energy.

Our culture has taught us to be defiantly opposed to facing how we're made— in the image of God, for relationship.

In the same way, we are taught to believe that if we can get stronger, smarter, or better, then our heart pain and problems will cease. We use our own gods (our own power) as the solution. This teaching of self-sufficiency only increases our frustration because it tells us to work harder to gain greater control, when we really need to be asking for help.

We don't know how to return to our hearts, and we don't know how to accept our own createdness. We're ashamed and terrified of being exposed as vulnerable creatures. Our culture has taught us to be defiantly opposed to facing how we're made—in the image of God, for relationship.

Our focus is the appetite of our stomachs. We find glory in whoever has the biggest house, the most prestigious job, the nicest car, the most talented children.

How do we get to the solution? How do we start to nourish the roots that give us full life? How do we experience the place of relationship? The solution is threefold.

First, we begin by feeling our feelings and exposing our hearts, thereby awakening our emotional and spiritual needs, desires, longings, and hope.

Second, we tell the truth about what is happening inside us. By acknowledging the content of our hearts, we expose how hungry we are for the vulnerable and authentic life of fullness. In doing so we begin stepping into the light of freedom.

Third, living out of our rediscovered freedom, we begin to grow more, recognizing our innate craving for full life and our inability to control it. In letting go of control, we ultimately find that *God is doing for us what we in our powerlessness cannot do.*

The Power of the Heart

A great story about the power of heart-filled life comes from a rural town in Tennessee. In this community there is an old, white-clapboard country church that was established in 1811.

In the graveyard beside it, a marker reads:

JOSIE TRIBLE

BELOVED WIFE OF J. M. ARMSTRONG

BORN MARCH 20, 1865

DEPARTED THIS LIFE JULY 5, 1890

AGED 25 YEARS, 3 MONTHS, 15 DAYS

While the words on this marker were somewhat common for their time, they speak simply and emphatically to how we are made.

The people of this era in rural Tennessee had very little control over diseases, disaster, and death. During a time when survival was a necessary focus of daily life, it was fairly common to bury someone long before what we think of as "their time." These people had the right to be calloused by the hardships of life. They knew powerlessness.

But instead of hiding their hearts' vulnerability, they were willing to experience the love of deep relationship through their powerlessness.

That plain marker speaks of a woman who died, leaving behind family. She was a woman who let herself be loved, and was so loved. Her husband called her "beloved." He dared speak the truth of his heart even in his loss.

I have counted the days of your life, my love. Before I knew or saw you, I held you sacred. I chose you and you chose me. Now, you are not with me. I count the days, 25 years, 3 months, 15 days, wishing that I could hold you one more time. I can't. But I love you, even now, knowing that all I can hold is the pain. I will live on but not forget you. I miss you. I love you.

Even though these words may not have been spoken, our hearts are made to speak them. Certainly, the words on the marker reveal the heart's potential during a time when one had the right not to live like that, considering all that daily life entailed.

If these people could have full life in the midst of their hardships, then how come we're not doing the same in our lives today? The answer is that we have lost contact with our hearts, and we don't dare take the risk of letting the power of love stretch beyond what we can control. Love was very much present, according to that grave marker. That's abundant living, full living. In spite of all the reasons to say, "I can't," the heart says, "I can."

QUESTIONS FOR PERSONAL REFLECTION

1. Remember a time when you experienced hope. Recalling this, what was frightening or painful to you about hope?

2. When you need to trust someone else, what do you feel?

3. What "counterfeit fulfillments" have you used to control and silence your heart's voice?

4. Can you remember a time when you wanted something so badly that your heart ached for it? What was it like desiring so much? Was that desire fulfilled? What did you feel?

5. What are some ways that you have tried to build self-esteem or make yourself worthy?

6. Many of us have been taught to believe that if we are "good enough," we will not have pain in our lives. In what ways do you try to be "good enough" to avoid pain? How did you learn this? Who taught you?

7. What memories do you have that make your heart feel full? What were some times that were especially fulfilling? What does your heart experience as you remember these times?

**For as he thinks in his heart,
so is he.**

—Proverbs 23:7 NKJV

CHAPTER 2

The
EIGHT FEELINGS

☙

You and I have only eight core feelings. We cannot live in fullness without knowing these feelings. The paradox is that if we choose fullness, we also choose to experience pain.

These are The Eight Feelings™:

- Hurt
- Lonely
- Sad
- Anger

- Fear
- Shame
- Guilt
- Glad

When talking about feelings, any words that are not these eight are a step away from the truth, a step away from the pure experience of the heart's depth, and a step away from how God made us. The Eight Feelings™ are the voice of the heart. You and I are born knowing and expressing them.

CONDITIONS OF THE HEART

Take a look at the list of conditions of the heart on pg. 162. They have feeling in them but aren't the feelings themselves.

When you begin to recognize and listen to your heart again, it will recognize you and guide you to the place where you can start to live life in openness. This openness will take you to fuller, richer living through relationship. To acknowledge that truth is to become vulnerable to your heart. Vulnerability exposes neediness, and neediness can lead us to seeking and knowing others and God.

Ultimately, unless we are capable of experiencing The Eight Feelings™ in their pure forms, we cannot truly express our needs, openly hunger in our desires, crave authentically in our longings, and passionately pursue hope.

The voice of the heart is always communicating to us. When the feelings are not exposed truthfully to ourselves, others, and God, the expression that occurs is impaired.

A FEW QUESTIONS

Ever since I began teaching about feelings and the Spiritual Root System™, people have asked some similar questions.

"Why is love not on the list?" Love is not on the list because love is so much more than a feeling. I would not dare minimize love's beauty and power to being only a feeling. Love has feelings in it, but love is more than a feeling.

"Depression is not a feeling?" No, depression is not a feeling, though people use it as one. It is a physiological state that also has feelings in it. Beyond physiology, depression often involves the depressing of feelings, especially anger.

Oftentimes, exposing and expressing the feelings of the heart alleviates depression. Blue, pleased, upset, happy, nervous—all of these are descriptions of feelings, but they're not feelings themselves. Anxiety, likewise, is not a feeling. In fact, depression and anxiety are often symptoms of avoiding true feelings, especially anger and fear. So to use these words is to distance ourselves from our own hearts.

"Why is only one feeling positive?" Actually, each feeling is positive because of where it can lead. There was a time when I thought, and had even been tutored to believe, that feelings are neither good nor bad; they just are. That is not true. All eight feelings are good. However, when I behave irresponsibly with my feelings, what I do with those feelings can certainly be evaluated. It's my behavior or planned behavior that is good or bad; feelings themselves are good—each feeling is a gift from God.

Each feeling has its own specific purpose in helping us live life fully. (See The Gift of Feelings Chart™ on pg. 157)

- **Hurt** leads to healing.
- **Loneliness** moves us to intimacy.
- **Sadness** expresses value and honor.
- **Anger** hungers for life.
- **Fear** awakens us to danger and begins wisdom.
- **Shame** maintains humility and mercy.
- **Guilt** brings forgiveness.
- **Gladness** proves hope of the heart to be true.

Gladness is at the bottom of the list for a reason. No one truly has the full assurance of what gladness brings until he or she is well versed in the other seven feelings.

The Eight Feelings™ are more like eyesight and thirst than they are like morality and behavior. No one is ashamed of waking in the morning, opening her eyes, and seeing. Very few of us end up thirsty midway through the day and say, "Oh, I'm such a bad, weak, stupid person because I need a glass of water."

Tragically, many of us have this experience with our hearts and say, "Oh, I'm a terrible person because I feel angry," or, "I feel lonely, so there must be something wrong with me." Many of us have been taught that feelings are bad. But we need to know that all eight feelings are good. Each feeling is given to us so that we may live life fully.

Feelings are the voice of the heart, and you will not have fullness until you're adept at hearing and experiencing all of them. When you are not aware of your feelings, your life is lived incompletely. Whenever you don't feel, you are blocked from living life to the fullest. Wherever you lack awareness of your heart, no room exists for God.

QUESTIONS FOR PERSONAL REFLECTION

1. What did your father teach you about your feelings? What did your mother teach you?

2. Are there any feelings that you have labeled as weak, wrong, or childish? If so how do you hide or avoid these feelings?

3. What do you need? What do you desire most deeply at this moment? What longings can you recognize in your self? What do you hope for?

4. How do you respond when someone you care for is disappointed? Do you try to "fix it" or make it better? Do you become angry? Do you become apathetic? Do you avoid the one in pain?

5. Do you say "I'm sorry" when you cry? For what are you apologizing?

6. Sometimes, in order to protect ourselves, we try to control the feelings of people we love. What are the ways that you try to prevent or manipulate others from feeling: hurt—sadness—loneliness—fear— anger— shame— guilt—gladness—

7. Sitting quietly in a chair with your feet on the floor, hands folded in your lap, listen. Listen to your heart intently for five minutes. What do you hear? Listen to your feelings, memories, pains, needs, longings, desires, hope.

I have heard your prayer,
I have seen your tears;
indeed, I will heal you.

—2 Kings 20:5

CHAPTER 3

HURT

☙

L ife is hard and life hurts. Hurt is the emotional and spiritual cry within us that lets us know that we have pain. It is the common thread that runs through all emotional and spiritual experiences.

It is the cry in your . . .

- loneliness that propels you to reach for deeper relationship.
- sadness that allows you to honor your losses with tears.
- fear that helps you see the condition of the world and find wisdom in spite of the heartaches.
- anger that propels you to pursue your passion.
- guilt that lets you seek reconciliation.
- shame that helps you know your place.
- gladness that allows you to find joy in the midst of life's transience.

No matter how thick or how high you may have built the walls around your heart, you are still susceptible to emotional and spiritual pain, certainly to wishing that the pain would end.

The experience of hurt, both by itself and as the thread that runs through all feelings, offers us a tremendous opportunity—the opportunity to admit, accept, and surrender to the truth of our neediness. Hurt exposes our desire to find healing for our pain. The acknowledgment of pain in turn awakens us to our true state as dependent, striving, trusting, curious, spontaneous, truthful creatures who prize life. Ironically, the admission of hurt acts as the catalyst to relief and healing of emotional and spiritual pain. Healing evokes and requires an admission of our vulnerability. Sticks and stones do savage our bodies, leaving us physically scarred, but it's the words that devastate our hearts.

Physically, if your leg is broken, you need a cast. The same is true emotionally and spiritually. If you are wounded by betrayal, for example, you need the time, attention, and nurturing of others to help you through. Hurt points to your need for help.

All our fixes—food, religion, sex, alcohol, illicit drugs, hard work, intelligence, prescription medications, discipline— won't mend our hearts.

All emotional and spiritual healing comes through relationship. This truth can be an obstacle to healing because the very thing that heals us (relationship) is the thing that previously wounded us. This paradox can lead us to defend against taking ownership of pain. We fear that our hearts will be wounded again. We escape pain by defending against the possibility of its recurrence.

Living in defensiveness neglects the heart—hurt is

emotional and spiritual internal bleeding that needs an emotional and spiritual solution. Defensiveness minimizes and denies the truth and seriousness of the pain of hurt.

HURT IS SEVERE

To show how severe hurt is, listen to the words we use to describe it. Notice how these phrases of violence work as admissions to the pain of emotional wounds:

- "It was like a spear in the chest."
- "It crushed me."
- "The rug was pulled out from under me."
- "I was stabbed in the back."
- "It was a blow to the gut."
- "I was blindsided."
- "It broke my heart."
- "It ripped me in two."
- "It tore me to pieces."

To minimize or deny the violence that we experience in hurt is to leave ourselves bleeding.

How many beatings can you endure, pretending they haven't even happened, before you become defended against how your heart is made?

Neglect of hurt through denial can lead us to worse consequences than the hurt itself. The very things we use to hide or numb hurt eventually kill our hearts. All our fixes— food, religion, sex, alcohol, illicit drugs, hard work, intelligence, prescription medications, discipline—won't mend our hearts. Our fixes do work against pain in that they mask or numb it enough to allow us to survive. But they will never bring true healing.

When we let go of the fixes that keep us numb, we begin to feel the pain of our wounds. We see that memories still carry pain, wounds from strained or broken relationships with loved ones still ache, intentions to offer love that were rejected still sting, and regrets about failing to love still twist our hearts in anguish. We keep trying to stifle the pain. In awakening to hurt, we see how susceptible we are to emotional and spiritual wounds, even those we believe we "should not have."

THE ADMISSION OF HURT

I remember my grandmother telling how she crouched in a corner across the room from her father and fourteen-year-old sister as her sister suffered her last breaths and died from typhoid fever. When she told me this story, my grandmother said, "That was just life back then." But the tears that ran down her eighty-eight-year-old face spoke the truth of her heart's pain. Her attempt to believe that "that's life" could not quite numb the hurt of seeing her sister die.

The painful memory of her sister was still stored in her heart. Seventy-six years later, she had not let herself feel it. She had resigned herself to the pain, but she had never accepted it. She had not grieved the hurt.

Admitting hurt brought the beginning of relief and some healing. She risked vulnerability as she was heard. In her vulnerability, she looked into faces that cared about her heart. That experience, in and of itself, is healing. She felt, spoke, and shared it with others.

Harm

Harm occurs when we emotionally and spiritually wound another in order to prevent feeling the pain in our own hearts. It is most often exhibited when we cross the boundaries of another without genuine regard, concern, or love for that person.

Hurt

Hurt is the emotional and spiritual experience that tells us we are feeling emotional and spiritual pain. In healthy relationships there is a willingness to allow someone to feel their own pain, because we have genuine regard, concern, and love for that person.

When you admit that life has *gotten to you* with words and deeds, you take a daring and courageous step. For in the admission of hurt, you also expose your wish for healing. To admit heart hurt is to begin to hope for heart solution, not just relief of the symptoms.

This hope (a search for a way through the pain) begins dismantling the walls of a defended life because in hoping and courageously risking, you have new experiences that validate your hope. Risking healing leads to new experiences (deeper relationships), making hope something to trust. New experiences then replace old experiences, proving hope to be true. This hope, when it leads to healing, helps tear down the walls of a defended heart.

When we tell the truth about hurt, others can help us heal. Healing sets us free from lowered expectations, counterfeit fulfillments, hopelessness, resignation, and toxic shame about how we are made.

RESENTMENT

We often attempt to avoid the truth and vulnerability of hurt by hiding it, denying it, or dying from it. We label hurt as an enemy and we become prideful and fearful of it. Examples abound, from alcoholism to eating disorders, compulsive materialism to glory-seeking, epicureanism to stoicism. While genetic predispositions can contribute, anything that we use to cover, deny, or destroy our emotional and spiritual hurt is detrimental to full life.

Avoiding hurt renders us numb and, therefore, numbs our hearts and their hunger for healing and life which comes through relationships.

Resentment is the product of trying to find solutions that reject hurt. When hurt is denied, minimized, or projected onto another, it becomes resentment. Through resentment we are able to deflect the focus from the internal pain and onto someone or something else. This impaired expression of hurt kills relationships and, therefore, stops all healing.

When we tell the truth about hurt, others can help us heal.

Healing comes through relationship of the heart. Resentment denies the heart.

In resentment, not only do I try to remove myself from the truth, but I also try to hide my resentment because it reveals that something has gotten to my heart—I'm vulnerable. This attempt to escape pain uses denial and blame to stave off vulnerability and, therefore, blocks the heart's experience of healing, forgiveness, acceptance, and love.

Resentment is unfortunately a logical and effective reaction to hurt. It justifies itself based upon the actions of another. Nursing a grudge generates its own energy because it keeps us from facing our own powerlessness over others and from accepting our vulnerability to pain. It is an attempt to have our cake and eat it, too.

Resentment allows us to know that we have pain, keep it secret, and find others to blame—making them responsible for fixing it. It even leads us in our denial to believe that if others would change, our hurt would be assuaged.

Resentment and Rejection

Consider the following example of the complexity of hurt and resentment. My spouse *finally* asks me, "What's wrong?" and I respond in a clear tone, "Nothing." This "nothing" exposes the nursing of a grudge that was a hurt but has now become a spear of resentment.

More clearly, the truth of what is going on inside me is that my wife asks, "What's wrong?" I lie and say, "Nothing." I seek to punish her by making her beg for relationship with me because I so despise the admission of my own hurt. I want *her* to figure it out. I want *her* to do the work. I want *her* to heal me (which she is neither able to do nor responsible for doing—that's God's business). In this instance, resentment has turned into a case against the person whom I have implicated as having "wronged" me.

In this denial or blame, we believe we have the right to act any way we want, because the other person deserves it. The "right" to act badly toward others because of our hurt is false justification. We hide our resentment by not acknowledging that we feel hurt. Resentment rejects those who reach toward us, and it becomes an intention to harm.

Sometimes the resentment we take out on another person is hurt we have never dealt with—a distrust in all others because of old, unhealed wounds. Other times the resentment is a refusal to feel hurt because life is just not the way we want it to be. We lack courage to face and feel life as it is. And other times we use resentment to stay stuck so we don't have to acknowledge our own vulnerability to and responsibility for our own hurt or hurt we have caused others.

When we are stuck in resentment toward another, we

Management

Management is an attempt to control life in order to stay safe and to make sure that outcomes we planned or predicted actually happen. When we manage a relationship, we prevent it from being an adventure, a joy, a surprise, and a gift.

———— ℭℜ ————

Mystery

Mystery is a willingness of heart to experience living truthfully and believe that we will find goodness in it. Living in mystery means walking in the faith that God is big enough to be in control, and that God doesn't require our help to get the job done.

don't want them to know that we harbor resentment, so we deny, manipulate, blame, and justify our behavior in order to hide or manage not only our hurt but now also our resentment. These behaviors take us farther from our hearts. In leaving our hearts, we leave behind full life. Until we stop resenting, start hurting, and take ownership of hurting others, we can never experience healing and full life.

It is my responsibility to deal truthfully with hurt. No amount of pretending, denying, or lying will change the truth.

THE GAIN OF HURT

Hurt is not just about what somebody did to me. It's about me taking ownership of how I feel about what happened to me. When I go to the doctor, and the doctor says, "Where does it hurt?" it's up to me to take ownership of putting my finger on the spot so that the doctor can do what the doctor does. Emotionally and spiritually, too, I need to take responsibility for my hurt in legitimate ways.

This responsibility does not mean that someone did not trigger our hurt. People say and do mean things—parents harm children, spouses abuse one another, friends betray confidences. Life and relationship hurt.

If we have influenced hurt that is harmful, we need to acknowledge it and seek forgiveness. Nevertheless, if we feel hurt, we need to lay claim to it and acknowledge it with a simple admission: "I hurt."

In order to have full life, we need to listen to our hurt and acknowledge our need for healing. The most intimate relationships are those in which we acknowledge to one another our vulnerability of hurt. "I've got a wound, and I need you to lean on," or "I need you to help me heal," or "I feel hurt when you _____."

Hurt moves the heart toward healing. Therefore, even if you're living in hurt, you are better off in the hurt than to not have it at all—to not feel is to not be alive, though sometimes being fully alive is excruciating.

Living in total awareness of your heart's experience of hurt, you realize the healing potential that has always been present. It is just that you have been unable or unwilling to risk receiving it. But when you reach out for someone to be with you, you become part of your own healing. Reaching to another and to God acknowledges your inability to heal alone, and in reaching you find care, assurance, and help in another.

Vulnerability to hurt initiates a balm for your pain. Willingness to surrender to pain begins healing. In admitting pain and reaching for help, you find healing. However, you need to reach to those who know the experience of hurt and healing themselves, not those in denial. After you have some healing, you might reach out to them.

This experience of hurting, reaching, and trusting nourishes your faith because it really makes you question whether or not God cares, and it exposes your hope that God will meet your needs. You step into the hope that *God can do for you what you cannot do.*

When you take part in relational hurting and healing with God and others, you find that restored hope leads to the truth of authentic faith—because you have actually experienced it. By trusting hope with action, you find healing experiences. These new experiences prove hope and trust to be valuable, real, and good. Hurting, reaching, and trusting create faith.

There is mysterious power in the fact that through the pain of hurt, you and I find deeper faith and greater strength.

QUESTIONS FOR PERSONAL REFLECTION

1. What are five of your most painful life events?

2. Who has hurt you most deeply? Have you told them? If not, what has stopped you?

3. How have your past hurts affected your ability to know and be known by others?

4. Have you ever had an experience when admitting your hurt lead to healing? If so, what happened? If not, what do you believe would happen if you were to do this?

5. What have you learned through emotional and spiritual pain?

6. Do you believe that the One that made your heart is great enough to heal its pain?

You make known to me the path of life;
You will fill me with joy in your presence,
with eternal pleasures at your right hand.

—Psalm 16:11

CHAPTER 4

LONELY

 C꙳

G od gave us loneliness so we would seek out relationship. Loneliness is a feeling that speaks to our deep hunger to belong and be known. We are often embarrassed or ashamed, or we believe there's something wrong with us for experiencing loneliness.

In truth, loneliness is the gift that speaks to how much is right with us while also pointing to how much has gone wrong. Because of loneliness, we inescapably desire relationship with ourselves, others, and God. Loneliness also points to how often we distance ourselves from all three vital forms of relationship.

RELATIONSHIP WITH SELF

Acknowledging loneliness allows me to see my heart and begin to know myself. It also allows me to see the hearts of others, and others to see my heart. This vulnerability is the foundation of intimate relationship. At the same time, loneliness exposes pain because it expresses how much I need what I hunger for.

Loneliness often speaks to our need to be with and know ourselves. It reveals our need for solitude. We learn through solitude that we need to stop activities in order to give ourselves a chance to hear our hearts and listen to what they are saying, sometimes waiting to get clarity. We do this through stopping, listening, waiting, resting, planting, and trusting.

We need to rest for the heart to regain strength, replenish hope, and prepare for the next step. We need to plant, tending to the seeds of desires, needs, longings, and hope within us. And we need to trust that we are emotional and spiritual creatures who need time out from the world's incessant urban clanging.

Valuing our loneliness through solitude does not necessarily lead to serenity. Sometimes we learn in loneliness to put our sword and shield down and cry our guts out about the battles we've waged and lost—dreams and hopes not fulfilled, friends missed, intimacies not honored, opportunities not taken, and struggles with God not seen through. But by struggling in solitude, we eventually rekindle the passion that led us into battle in the first place.

RELATIONSHIP WITH OTHERS

Another expression of loneliness identifies our hunger for the intimacy of community.

- "Will you be with me?"
- "Can we spend time together?"
- "Can you listen to my pain?"
- "Will you pray for me?"
- "Will you stand up for me?"

Loneliness pushes me to seek to be known. There's a limit to how long I can stand being around others without being known.

Demand

Demand seeks to fulfill needs through our power over others. Demand leaves no room for choice by the other person; therefore, the love we receive is forced and can't be given from the heart of the other person. Love is always a gift given freely without merit. Demanding people expose a distrustful, wounded heart. They believe that no one could truly love them for themselves.

Expectation

Expectation is a desire to live in hope and yet a willingness to hear, "No." Expectant people tell the truth, make choices, and trust others and themselves. People of expectation understand that God is not demanding, but is highly expectant. They understand that God does not wish for their subordination, but that He desires the surrender of their hearts.

For instance, have you ever been to a dinner party where you don't really know the people? You mingle, smile, eat, visit, but you can't wait to get home and spend time with your spouse, your children, or your friends. You want to be where you can put your elbows on the table and just talk and laugh. The people who know you already accept you as you are, so you leave that situation highly replenished. Even if you are at a banquet as the recipient of an award, you may be more replenished by eating with your buddies than you would be by receiving a coveted prize.

Loneliness arouses an emotional and spiritual hunger to be received, known, and loved by another. It is a hunger to be accepted as we are. If we are accepted and enjoyed for who we truly are, then we cannot help but find replenishment. We will likewise be filled emotionally and spiritually. We will be compelled to share our passion for life and do good things through relationship with others.

RELATIONSHIP WITH GOD

The heart also voices a kind of loneliness that can never be completely filled, answered, or quieted as long as we live. This loneliness awakens us to our emotional and spiritual longing for God.

Have you ever seen a sunset that struck your heart with its strength of color spread all over the sky and ground? The part of you that is struck by such movement and beauty is the same part that aches with the recognition of how incomplete you are. In the aching, your heart recognizes the need for the One who made it.

This loneliness for more goodness and fullness quite often comes in moments of celebration—a child's birth, a twenty-fifth anniversary, a graduation, a marriage. The goodness of celebration, which must be felt to be truly known, will end. In our hearts we want to go where the wonder, celebration, passion, and relational fulfillment never stop. We want to go to the source of this goodness.

Loneliness renders us vulnerable to our hunger for emotional and spiritual fulfillment, thus exposing us to all relationship needs.

When my oldest son was about three, I remember showing him his first rainbow. Instead of stopping in the wonder of it, he began walking toward it, saying, "Take me there, Daddy." His heart was lonely, longing to be more a part of the beauty. He valued it. When he found out that I couldn't take him there, he ached in his waiting for what he could not completely have, but what he knew he was made for.

Loneliness renders us vulnerable to our hunger for emotional and spiritual fulfillment, thus exposing us to all relationship needs. But in a world that screams negativity about dependency and glorifies self-sufficiency, loneliness is the feeling that we work hardest to avoid. The irony is that the more we work to avoid it, the more it occurs. And the more we work to hide it, the more we miss out on life.

Loneliness is gratified only in intimacy. Without admitting loneliness, we are destined to remain in deep emotional and spiritual conflict. If we don't address it, loneliness never stops whispering to us in the quiet moments, "something is missing." So instead of filling our hunger with authentic relational sustenance, we feed our hearts junk that relieves instead of fills.

If we have courage enough to walk into the spirituality of loneliness, we will awaken to how good God is and how much we are dependent on that goodness and the goodness of the One who shapes children's hearts.

A lot of us make sure that we live intense lives to keep from facing our hunger for intimacy. We maintain activities and acquaintances that feel like closeness. But those relationships are our way of avoiding the pain of hope and our fear of dependence, which are the foundations of intimacy.

The same can be true of settled lives of habitual routine, in which intimacy appears to exist because no one dares address their hearts openly.

Many of us come from places where living from our hearts is dangerous, so painful that survival requires that we try to reject our hearts. Relational wounds leave us in conflict—deeply ashamed of our hunger for intimacy indicated by loneliness, and at the same time, deeply craving relationship with others because we have so missed intimacy in our growing up.

For those of us from these childhoods, the most difficult experience in adulthood is to acknowledge our loneliness and be intimate with another person without demanding that they stop our heart's pain. To be close in adulthood is to fully awaken to our heart's pain and even contempt for the loneliness of our past.

In this conflicted, painful loneliness, we usually blame

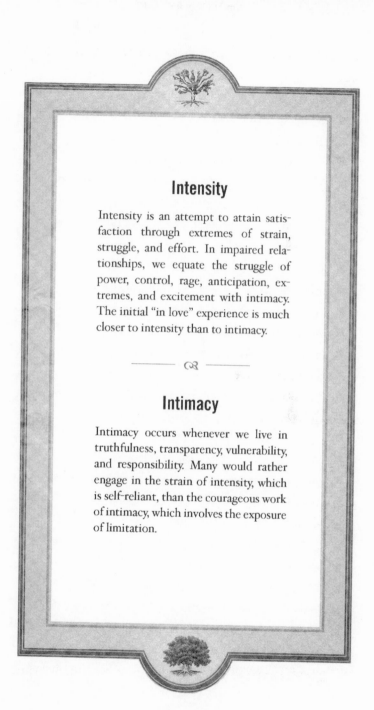

Intensity

Intensity is an attempt to attain satisfaction through extremes of strain, struggle, and effort. In impaired relationships, we equate the struggle of power, control, rage, anticipation, extremes, and excitement with intimacy. The initial "in love" experience is much closer to intensity than to intimacy.

Intimacy

Intimacy occurs whenever we live in truthfulness, transparency, vulnerability, and responsibility. Many would rather engage in the strain of intensity, which is self-reliant, than the courageous work of intimacy, which involves the exposure of limitation.

the way we are made more than we give responsibility to the ones who wounded us.

We blame ourselves, diminishing our hearts' desires and feelings in order to belong. We construct false selves so that others will love us.

This impaired expression of loneliness is tragic because it is an attempt to belong and to be intimate by not living truthfully from the heart. The "love" we receive is for behaving falsely, and we secretly, shamefully believe that we made someone love us.

How many times have you tried to find acceptance by pretending to enjoy something that you didn't like? From where we work to who we marry, from where we worship to what we wear, from what we drive to where we live, these are all expressions of emotional and spiritual values. If they do not reflect who we legitimately are (or desire to be), they are forms of falsehood that corrupt the character of who we are made to be.

APATHY

We often try to negate our desire to be in relationship with others because of woundedness. In this state, loneliness instigates a sense of being threatened. We disregard, minimize, or defeat our hunger for intimacy—our wish to love and be loved—and in its place we experience its impairment: apathy. Apathy is the opposite of love. It denies our loneliness and thus our need for intimate relationship.

Many of us incorrectly believe that hate is the opposite of love. Hate is actually the passion of love that has been twisted against itself. Hatred exposes the depth of a wound and acts as a way to deny the hurt and sadness of how much something matters.

Apathy, on the other hand, is our defiant attempt to deny the existence of the heart. The degree to which we have put apathy in the place of loneliness is the degree to which we place ourselves as separate from humanity and God.

The degree to which we have put apathy in the place of loneliness is the degree to which we place ourselves as separate from humanity and God.

Apathy makes us inhuman because it rejects our emotional and spiritual makeup. In the inhumanity of apathy we become like the great white shark that swims the ocean and consumes whatever is in its path. It does not care about what it devours. It simply takes without regard. It does not love or hate. It does not care.

In rediscovering our God-made loneliness, we need to take ownership of how we attempt to escape, attack, or manipulate the heart's makeup. Here are some ways that we avoid intimacy or truth in relationship and move into apathy:

- "I don't care."
- "It doesn't matter."
- "Whatever."
- "There are plenty of fish in the sea."
- "What's the difference?"
- "OK, fine, that works for me."

Apathy is our only defense against the acknowledgment of our true dependency and the recognition of our hope for intimacy. Many survivors fight to the death—using power, achievement, alcohol, control, isolation—to maintain apathy and to avoid caring. They do all this to block the exposure of their hearts.

Apathy is the opposite of love. Loneliness acknowledges the need for love. Apathy attempts to negate it.

Unacknowledged loneliness makes orphans of us all. All we get for surviving our loneliness rather than using its gifts is its results—we wind up alone.

THE GIFT OF LONELINESS

Based upon the painful experience that made you a survivor, you have the right to remain defended. But if you will only risk giving up that right, you stand to gain *everything for which your heart hungers.*

By surrendering to the truth that we are made for relationship, we find the very things we thought we could never have—closeness, warmth, tenderness, intimacy, and love with ourselves, others, and God.

QUESTIONS FOR PERSONAL REFLECTION

1. How much time do you spend alone? Do you find this time replenishing?

2. What is the difference between isolation and solitude? Would you describe your alone time as isolation or solitude?

3. Think of a time when, in your loneliness, you longed for something, someone, or someplace. Describe it.

4. What is your mind's picture of a person who feels lonely? Are you ashamed of feeling lonely? If so, what has led you to this belief?

5. What are you lonely for today? What is threatening to you about acknowledging this loneliness?

6. What do you do to avoid feeling lonely?

7. How do you fulfill your need for relationship and your desire for intimacy?

Sorrow is better than laughter,
for by sadness of countenance
the heart is made glad.

—Ecclesiastes 7:3 NRSV

CHAPTER 5

SAD

༄

If you wish to experience life to the fullest, your heart requires that you be willing to feel sadness. Sadness is the feeling that speaks to how much you value what is missed, what is gone, and what is lost. It also speaks of how deeply you value what you love, what you have, and what you live.

Sadness is proportional—the more sadness you feel after a loss, the more you value what is lost. The more you live an openhearted life of fullness, the more you lose. Sadness gives us the gift of valuing and honoring life.

When I die, I hope there will be a lot of people and great sadness at my funeral. I want people to weep about my being gone. I want them to cry because the man they knew is no longer with them. I want them to say that I was known, that I was loved, that I *mattered*. And while they are honoring my life with their tears, they will be honoring their own hearts even more because they have opened their hearts to being known.

Their tears will express the state of their hearts and allow them to recognize that they do indeed *matter* to themselves and to a relationship that was important. They allowed me, as someone they loved, to get to them; they allowed themselves to be vulnerable by acknowledging that they could love.

Sadness is the loving feeling because it expresses value and honor for something or someone gone or lost. Sadness is for wealthy-hearted people.

THE GIFT OF SADNESS

One of the gifts of sadness is that it is the first step toward healing from loss. Sadness speaks directly to our need to grieve for what is gone. If we grieve genuinely, we eventually come to accept life on life's terms. Through grief, we find comfort and deeper wisdom as we move about in life in the absence of who or what was lost. From that acceptance we find healing.

Sadness is fundamental to full life because it opens the door to healing. However, if we can't acknowledge how much what we've lost means to us, then sadness will deepen because the need to honor our losses with grief doesn't go away.

Many of us have heard that we need to disregard our losses and dismiss the pain of our hearts. People say, "Don't cry over spilled milk," or "That fire has already burned," or "That's water under the bridge."

Have you ever wondered what happens to all the water after it passes "under the bridge"? In my own recovery of heart, I got off the bridge and walked along the riverbank, following the river to its end. I could hardly believe what I found. All that water, from all those years, that I thought had flowed to the ocean or evaporated, had collected in a big pool at the base of a dam. Only so much water can flow under that bridge before the dam will crack and break from the strain. The danger isn't in releasing the water—the danger is in *never* releasing the water.

Resignation

Rooted in hopelessness, resignation is an attempt to escape and refuse to feel emotional and spiritual pain. In resignation, we feign acceptance of life issues that are very painful and unresolved. We use resignation to avoid dependency, neediness, and vulnerability because we see these experiences as weaknesses.

———— ℀ ————

Acceptance

Acceptance is having emotional and spiritual serenity about a situation that we can't do anything about. It comes through the willingness to grieve and is a result of working through the pain of life problems, in hope that good will come. Acceptance is rooted in the certainty that comes from experiencing the truths of the heart.

The heart's sadness is the same way. Either we value life and deal with the losses we have experienced, or they will eventually burst open and deal with us as consequences that occur due to denial of grief. If we dare listen to our sadness and value the losses it declares, we will awaken to the restoring power of grief. Grief, in turn, leads us to acceptance.

SELF-PITY

Our society often views people who express sadness as being stuck in self-pity. To avoid this label, we often hide our sadness behind a facade of false strength or deny it to those with whom we have relationship. We equate sadness with weakness, lack of dependability, or even faithlessness.

Sadness and self-pity, however, differ greatly—the distance between them is the distance across the widest chasm of the Grand Canyon. Self-pity is a way to avoid genuine sadness. It is a series of dialogues that go something like: "Nothing ever goes right for me; no matter how much I try, things still turn out badly." Or, "I'm always the one who has to sacrifice." When we experience self-pity, we are unwilling to feel sadness. Rather, we use self-pity to defend against our sadness and avoid exposing our hearts.

Self-pity is a way to escape the pain of sadness by trying to make others feel sadness for us. I might look at you and say, "You know, no matter how much I try, nothing goes well for me. Every time I turn around something else goes wrong. You know I try! You've seen me. I'm working as hard as I can! What else can I do? I may as well just give up! It's no use!"

I'm attempting to express the truth of my heart—I am sad—but I am unwilling to let myself feel sad, so I try to make you feel what I refuse to feel. I try to make you feel the sadness that I need to feel for myself. I try to make you value me so I don't have to value myself.

Self-pity is an attempt to manipulate others into taking responsibility for our heart's response and neediness. It's an attempt to be valued, but with others doing all the work. Because we have been taught to mistake sadness for self-pity, we often dismiss our need to feel sadness as something to be hidden or denied in an attempt to block the appearance of self-pity.

Self-pity is a way to escape the pain of sadness by trying to make others feel sadness for us.

Think about how often you have said to yourself, "It's no big deal. I will just get over it."

I've even heard people say, "She has a tremendous amount of faith, a tremendous amount of trust in God. She didn't shed a tear at her own son's funeral."

That's considered strong faith, to not have pain over your son's death? That's not faith. It's being terrified of feeling. That is the way of woundedness and survival, of rejecting our humanity and the struggle of relational intimacy with God.

A CLEANSING FEELING

When we cannot feel sadness, when we cannot value, when we cannot ache within over what we lose, we have resigned ourselves to an existence that never lets life affect us. As a result, we can never find the healing that sadness can bring.

Because sadness is a cleansing feeling, it eases the burden of daily life. Tears are gifts that we give to whatever we lose.

THE GAIN OF SADNESS

A couple of years ago, my friend's mother died of cancer. She lived two years after her initial diagnosis. I had known her since I was seven. Five minutes before she died, she spoke to her husband: "We have had a good life together . . . two children, healthy grandchildren. I always loved you, before you even knew. I can't hang on anymore. Let me go." He did. He loved her deeply. She died. In his willingness to feel all of his sadness, by letting her go he was truly able to value her completely. He also valued the love he had for her.

The day of her funeral I waited in line for more than an hour and a half just to get into the funeral home to see the family. Many people came to grieve the death of this woman and honor her life. This lady, mother, wife, was in no clubs, was not written up in the newspaper until her obituary, spoke at no banquets, held no position of power, yet when she died, I could hardly get into the building to say good-bye.

I remember the beauty of her life and how easily she could laugh at our childhood antics. I also remember her willingness to make chocolate chip cookies. She loved and was known simply for love. She loved living. I cry even now at her memory. I value her and miss her. I'm glad I can.

Life is not a dress rehearsal for someday when it will become real. We are living our lives now, not practicing for a life to come.

We need to be willing to value openly and have deep sadness.

We need to write poems and songs. We need to send letters to our children at the occasions of their milestones, raise grandchildren to the stars for God to see, hug our friends and tell them how much we love them.

We need to take time to visit on the porch with someone who dropped by, visit old friends we've been meaning to see, get up early to listen to God whisper glorious things as the sun rises.

We need to climb these heights and take on all kinds of journeys as a way to live.

And we need to grieve deeply when people we love depart or when what we dream doesn't come true.

We cannot delight deeply in anything or anyone unless we are willing to walk in the world of sadness. Sadness allows the intimacy and impact of love to be much richer because it exposes the heart to its true ability to value and honor.

What are you sad about? What wound has been unable to heal because of the sadness you aren't feeling? What sadness is in your life that you fight against? What have you been dreaming of doing that you haven't risked because you might lose?

QUESTIONS FOR PERSONAL REFLECTION

1. What have been your three greatest losses?

2. What do you deeply wish for that you do not have?

3. How do you express disappointment? Do you honor your disappointments with sadness? What makes grieving your losses so important?

4. When was the last time you sincerely cried for something? Were you ashamed of your tears? What do you believe about tears?

5. Who is the person in your life that you miss the most? For whom do you not feel sadness, but wish you could?

6. When you remember times that are past (childhood, college, the "good old days," etc.), do you honor these times with sadness or do you avoid remembering them? How have you honored or avoided them?

7. Do you feel more deeply watching television or movies than you do with real life? What do these feelings show you about your heart?

8. How do you show people you care about them?

Delight yourself in the LORD**,
and he will give you the
desires of your heart.**

—Psalm 37:4

CHAPTER 6

ANGER

CR

I grew up believing that anger was a destructive force to avoid. That if I ever felt anger, I had somehow fallen short. Either I had not been patient enough, or I had let others see they had "gotten to me." I thought that I was experiencing a failure of character. Anger was something to withhold, hide, or use to keep others away from my vulnerability. This impaired belief taught me how to deny my heart's true construction and allowed me to live a life of counterfeit fulfillment.

In truth, anger is possibly the most important feeling we experience as emotional and spiritual beings because it is the first step to authentic living. It shows our yearning and hunger for life.

Anger helps us pursue full life by exposing the substance, desires, and commitments of our hearts.

Anger works to enhance relationships by building bridges of intimacy with others. You know who you're in relationship with, their desires, their transparency and authenticity. Angry people can be known because of their unwillingness to hide.

THE HEART'S SUBSTANCE

In exposing the heart's substance, anger helps us in two ways:

1. It shows the presence of passion.
2. It indicates the experience of other feelings.

Words we don't often associate with anger are *yearning, wishing, hungering,* and *desiring.* Anger is the energy of desire and the willingness to reach for the desire to be satisfied. It shows us, even comforts us with, what we care about.

Authentic anger is a *caring* feeling, telling us that something matters.

Authentic anger is a *caring* feeling, telling us that something matters. In fact, the energy of compassion is rooted in anger, the desire to make the pain we feel and see come to an end.

Anger exposes what we value and expresses our willingness to do what is required to reach that value. It allows us to stay with our values, take sides, and even die for what we believe in.

Jesus, who turned the tables over in the temple and drove out thieves from a sacred place, experienced true anger. He showed the vulnerability of full passion and compassion, the desire to make what had become rotten pure again.

This expression of anger is the same that occurs when marital infidelity is exposed or recommitment to love occurs after betrayal. It is the risk of telling the truth or just doing a courageous act.

Responsibility *for* another

Responsibility for another assumes that a person's inability requires us to decide for him or her. Little children and old people need loving caregivers to be responsible for them. However, we are not responsible for other adults. In order to hide our fear of facing our heart's truths and our individual journey, we try to manipulate others into taking responsibility for us.

———— ∞ ————

Responsibility *to* another

Responsibility to another person is a form of love and respect. We are responsible to others when we speak truth from our hearts, but we leave others to decide for themselves, knowing that their life is their own. Responsibility to others recognizes their capabilities and at the same time our need for help.

Besides showing the presence of passion, anger indicates the experience of other feelings. Anger can indicate the need to stop and consider what is happening inside of us. Anger, therefore, becomes a warning signal, telling us to look inside at what fear, hurt, sadness, or loneliness we are experiencing.

Anger also indicates a need to take responsibility for other feelings. Thus, anger will help identify losses (sadness), rejections (loneliness), wounds (hurt), or limitations (fear) and give us the opportunity to tell the truth about what is really going on inside our hearts.

Anger is the energy that allows us to admit these other feelings. It gives us vitality—the guts to confess, admit, or "show up."

The Separation Emotion

Anger is also the energy that compels us to expose our choices and truths. Anger reveals what matters to us. When something matters to us, we are willing to make choices and commitments.

For example, Mother Teresa saw the people she loved being counted as nothing, allowed to die without hope, nurturing, or care. In passion and compassion—in true anger from her heart—she reached out to make a difference in these people's lives. She followed her desire to serve "worthless" people, separating herself, identifying herself, and becoming an example of a life lived truthfully and openly.

From Mother Teresa's passionate life of service to exposing a hurt about what someone said to us this morning, anger is the emotion of self-identity that motivates us to make commitments and follow through because we desire to do so. It is the energy that compels us to act. We do not act out of obligation; we act out of true choice.

As the self-identity emotion, anger tells me where I stop and where you start because anger exposes and expresses the heart's desires and true content. This exposure separates and declares our intentions—makes known our choices, decisions, values, feelings, and needs.

Anger creates identity. Through it, we are known.

Anger, then, is the feeling that clarifies who we are and who we are not. By making us known, anger pushes us to be truthful, and therefore trustworthy. If we can say "no" (be truthful), then the truthfulness of our "yes" has great value. We can be depended upon because of our anger.

Our ability to show our true identity makes us available for relationship; in fact, anger reaches out for it. And when we reach out in truth and the reaching is met by another in truth, we build authentic relationships.

IMPAIRED ANGER

Anger's impaired states, depression and pride, express contempt for our passion and vulnerability. Depression pushes passion back into the heart. Pride denies the vulnerability revealed in anger. Both impaired states are attempts to fight the heart's powerful desire for life, which is clearly revealed in anger.

Depression

In depression, we turn against ourselves and have contempt for our hearts. We force our fight for life to be still and our cry for identity to be silent. All this energy turned against the self wears us out.

Depression rejects the experience of our yearnings and wishes for things to be different. It's a denial of the heart's desire to reach out.

Depression is the nonexposure experience. It keeps our passions at bay so that we don't expose the wishes revealed in our vulnerability. It says to our hearts, "What's the use?"

If I am depressed, I close off my desires—the desire to get up, to eat, to take a bath, to go for a walk, to care—I close off my hunger for life. This state of depression is directly related to avoided anger, which takes us away from dealing with deeper sadness, loneliness, hurt, or fear.

In *It's a Wonderful Life*, George Bailey stood on the bridge on Christmas Eve in a world that had become dark for him. He was angry at his dreams, contemptuous of his hope for goodness, and hopeless about his passion for his own and others' well-being. He despised and then depressed his ache for life, finally trying to conclude that it was useless—wishing that he had never been born.

When Clarence, George's guardian angel, jumped into the water, George instantly responded from his true heart, throwing himself into the water to save another human being. He couldn't stop being George—courageous of heart and full of desire and passion. He couldn't stop being who God made him to be.

The rest of the movie is about George's struggle to accept his passion, vulnerability, and hope—and how these things deeply matter. The return of his desire for life, his anger turned outward, reignites the dedication and devotion to what he believes. It eventually takes him home, willing to face any conse-quences for love's sake. He finally learns to accept love and give love. Desire reawakened is rooted in the feeling of anger.

Pride

Pride keeps us from abundant living because it rejects our powerlessness. Pride refuses to believe that life is bigger than we are and that life affects us. If we avoid our anger, we can deny our vulnerability, and thus our hunger to overcome ob-stacles that block the desires of our hearts.

Pride keeps us from abundant living because it rejects our powerlessness.

When we attempt to deny our vulnerability, we use the energy of anger to build a wall around the heart which we believe will stop or relieve life's pains. Unfortunately, this lack of courage to meet life on its own terms also blocks our recognition of the heart's miraculous abilities.

One such ability is the capacity to hope in spite of the appearance of defeat.

Another is the power to reach out in vulnerability, though we have every reason to wish not to ever hurt again. Another is our propensity to comfort another who previ-ously harmed us but has now sought forgiveness.

These abilities, fueled by anger, all affirm our poten-tial for relational intimacy. Each situation also requires that we use anger to push aside pride's wall in order to ad-mit vulnerability.

A wall of pride around the heart blocks anger because pride says:

- "It didn't bother me."
- "I'm tougher than that."
- "You don't get to me."
- "I don't need anyone."
- "I can handle it."
- "I can take whatever you dish out."

Pride also blocks our need to admit the failure of self-sufficiency because pride cannot admit fault. Pride does not allow us to seek forgiveness ("I didn't do anything") or forgive others ("It didn't bother me"). Through pride, we justify our behaviors instead of accepting responsibility. We use pride to block the truth of the harm we cause. Through pride, we avoid the truth of our own limitations, susceptibility to problems, and vulnerability to pain.

Until we truly feel our own pain by recognizing that life gets to our hearts, we cannot meet others in their pain. If we cannot empathize, we can never be close to another or have involvement in a cause greater than ourselves (even if that cause is intimate relationship).

Anger, the desire for full life, allows us to stand in truth, while pride entices us to stand in arrogance. How many relationships have you seen come to an end because the individuals were unwilling to be angry enough to care and build a bridge?

THE GAIN OF ANGER

Anger, then, creates movement. It expresses our desire for life and helps us move into and remain present in the desires we are made for. Anger tells the truth about our hearts' yearnings without the intention to harm.

Angry people who are pure with their anger can be good company to keep. Moses was angry. Abraham Lincoln was angry. Martin Luther King Jr. was angry. Each of them brought personal, powerful passion and vulnerability to life. All of them walked with their faces set on the path of their desires. Each of them expressed a clear identity, rejected pride, emerged from depression, trusted God, and stepped into full life.

QUESTIONS FOR PERSONAL REFLECTION

1. Who or what are you angry with? How is this anger related to your desires?

2. Have you ever been angry with God? What about? What did you most desire at those times? Were those desires fulfilled? What do you feel about that?

3. How can anger move you towards fulfilling your heart's passions?

4. Think of a time that you were depressed. What were you angry about that you could not express?

5. What differences do you see between anger and rage? What were some times when you acted out of rage? Did the outcomes provide heart gratification or leave you wanting more? Did they leave you confused or empty? Explain.

6. What role does anger play in integrity? What are some ways that anger has contributed to your personal integrity?

7. How can your anger help you declare your heart's truths?

**The fear of the Lᴏʀᴅ is
the beginning of wisdom.**

—Psalm 111:10

CHAPTER 7

FEAR

☞

Fear brings us strength. It is the feeling that allows us to experience risk, trust, dependency, collaboration, and, ultimately, wisdom because it helps us realize our need for help.

This statement may sound contrary to everything you've ever heard about fear. For many of us, fear equals weakness or we see it as an influence that makes us act in doubt and distrust in relationship, which makes us hide our fear. In our fear of fear, we continually demand guarantees and are overly controlling in any risk we take.

But if we admit our fear, it can produce remarkable benefits. We discover that fear can be about assertion and prevention. If in the face of fear, we can recognize our need for help, we find great opportunity.

Fear can motivate you to reach out for help, risk your heart with your need, and trust others for assistance. Fear can help you depend upon others for their skill and willingness, and can help you collaborate with others for mutual gain. If you express fear truthfully, you can gain wisdom through the experience.

Unfortunately, too many of us answer fear by silencing its voice. We run from risk, eliminate trust, hide our dependency, and become fretful and controlling about collaboration. Fear offers the opportunity to trust God and others with our need for help, or it entices us to stay stuck in distrust and self-will.

Acknowledging our fear offers new relational experiences and initiates the beginning of wisdom. Wisdom is essential to full life, and it begins by listening to fear. Wisdom develops from a keen understanding of human nature coupled with a deeply experienced awareness of spiritual truth. That was what Jesus meant when He called us to become both innocent as doves and cunning as serpents. If we have only a keen understanding of human nature, then all we have is common sense, the "street smarts" that help us survive by manipulation. This savvy makes all relationships about quid pro quo rather than about true intimacy.

If we have only a deep awareness of spiritual truth, then we will not have the sense to know the difference between an animal that is wounded or one that is rabid. This naiveté makes us foolish and a danger to ourselves and others.

But to join the two is to choose to live from the heart and face new experiences with discernment and passion rather than cynicism or sentimentality.

FEAR'S GIFT IS WISDOM

Wisdom begins its creation through fear. Here is how.

Fear awakens us to danger. It is a visceral reaction to physical threat, but more important, because we are creatures of the heart, fear alerts us to emotional and spiritual danger.

When we are around someone who is sarcastic or belittling, for example, our hearts beat with caution. When we are around someone who we suspect will reject us in meanness, our hearts anticipate a wound, allowing us to behave carefully.

These are emotional and spiritual fear responses. By the very fact of our watchfulness, we recognize inside ourselves a personal worth. By listening to our fear, we recognize our value and prepare to prevent harm to ourselves and others. We are developing wisdom—a keen sense of human nature and a deep awareness of the spiritual.

Acknowledging our fear offers new relational experiences and initiates the beginning of wisdom.

This caution affords us discernment, which gives us a sense of others' intentions and recognition of our own. Fear is not to help us move from discernment to judgment.

Judgment hides fear. It is a form of stopping fear without listening to it. It keeps us from hearing the meaning of our fear in the moment when we are experiencing it.

Discernment that comes by listening to our fear helps us choose the wisest course of action, one that takes into account our propensity to harm others and values our potential to love.

Fear offers us the chance to decide or discern which direction to go. When we move into life, we can risk truth and recognize potential harm. Or as survivors we can hide by pretending fear isn't happening or by attacking the potential harm.

THE COST OF CHOICES

To keep us from danger, fear allows us to count the cost of our choices, and it instigates the recognition of potential consequences. "If I go down that path, I could get lost." The fear does not necessarily make us change our behavior (anger is the action emotion), but it makes us aware of our choices. If we are not able or willing to listen to this fear, we become foolish or fearless (oblivious to danger), or cowardly and avoidant (unwilling to face danger).

If we don't count the cost of our actions, then we declare ourselves unworthy of trust. If we reject ownership of the heart's truth and fail to take responsibility for it, then we surely aren't going to care for others. If the competent leaders, parents, and companions have healthy fear, they will attract others because in their fear they have assessed the situation, considered the possibilities, and they are attempting to respond in wisdom. They have become dependable and trustworthy by listening to and learning from healthy fear.

Listening to and valuing fear helps you prepare for the challenge of attaining the desires of your heart. When you truly desire something you do not have, you automatically experience fear. This fear concerns the possibilities of failure, pain, humiliation, disappointment, and loss. If your desire is fixed, your fear is a tool that helps you initiate plans and practice—fear makes you do the work of preparation, getting ready for the challenge.

All true soldiers spend a great deal of time preparing for battle. The fear that leads to preparation helps the soldiers become fully equipped to go out and do a task that could cost them their lives and the lives of others. The fear

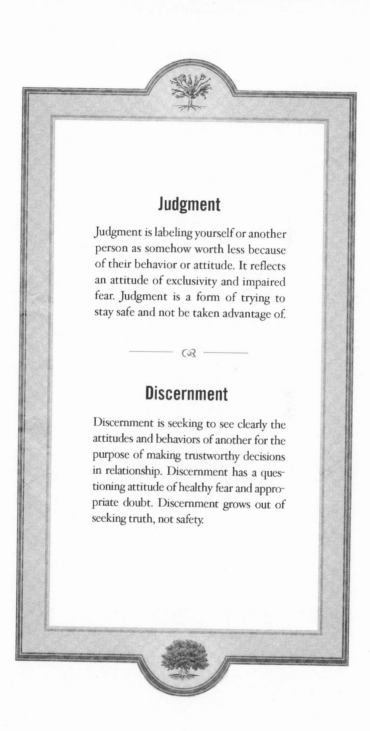

Judgment

Judgment is labeling yourself or another person as somehow worth less because of their behavior or attitude. It reflects an attitude of exclusivity and impaired fear. Judgment is a form of trying to stay safe and not be taken advantage of.

———— ∽ ————

Discernment

Discernment is seeking to see clearly the attitudes and behaviors of another for the purpose of making trustworthy decisions in relationship. Discernment has a questioning attitude of healthy fear and appropriate doubt. Discernment grows out of seeking truth, not safety.

that helps soldiers prepare originates in the desire to serve nobly and give to one's people. In this way fear sheds light on our desires and is the first step in making them come true.

This truth applies to all noble soldiers, scientists, ballplayers, physicians, pastors, parents—all of us. As we acknowledge dangers, count costs, and prepare for challenges as a response to fear, we stand face-to-face with a paradox.

We are personally responsible for making choices, yet we cannot succeed alone. We are limited, yet we will forever find that great strength lies in relying upon one another. Depending is good. We don't have enough knowledge, wisdom, or power to succeed alone, yet we are completely responsible for all of our choices.

FACING RESPONSIBILITY

Regardless of our fear of failure, rejection, humiliation, love, or success, we discover that accepting responsibility for our hearts' desires can be scary.

That we dare to act at all, knowing that we are responsible for our hearts, shows how courageous it is to take ownership of responsibility. Courage is about facing responsibility and telling the truth about ourselves—successes and failures.

Fear makes us face ourselves and reveals our neediness. In facing ourselves, we come to terms with how deeply limited we are and how prone we are to attack others as a way to get control over our own limitations instead of letting our limitations lead us to help. However, in admitting our situations, we have the opportunity to grow beyond them.

When we see our limitations, we begin to see how much we need others in order to succeed in making good, true, noble, helpful choices about living. By coming to terms with fear, we can take ownership of it and begin to be more truthful in our relationships. If we accept and use the benefits of fear, we discover that: (1) we live fully by being responsible, and (2) we are capable of living successfully by accepting our limitations and our need for others.

Fear makes us face ourselves and reveals our neediness.

My limitations give others appropriate influence or authority in my life. In this circumstance I need to submit to the other's teaching for my benefit. Likewise, when other people admit their limitations, they give me an opportunity to help.

Healthy fear leads me into relationship because it helps me recognize that I am not enough. I need others. I need others who have skills and substance different from my own.

This fear is a clear recognition of my heart's need to follow and respect the appropriate authority of someone who has what I do not have. Fear allows me to be willing to listen to the wisdom of others and acknowledge their talents.

Transforming Truth

By awakening to our need for help and asking for it, we are reaching into the hope that someone has answers and has the heart's desire to offer them. We have to have somewhere to go in our dependency and limitations, so our fear leads us to risk trusting others, which in turn can deepen our relationships by exposing who we are and where we genuinely struggle. Ultimately, through fear, we realize that we are personally responsible for seeing how needy we are.

When we accept this fact, either we can behave truthfully in our neediness, or we can continue to defend and pretend, which requires old survival behavior and counterfeit fulfillment. The benefit of awareness and truthfulness is that you and I see that no one is the king or queen. In fact, each of us is royalty and servant. Each of us has value—each has gifts and the need to give them.

The gift of recognizing our limitations is that through our neediness we receive many benefits—knowledge, experience, truth, ability, understanding, and the desire to give away what we have already received.

This paradox—that *in our weakness begins our strength, in our fear begins our wisdom*—is transforming truth.

Borrowing Trouble

Ironically, coming to grips with fear is a scary thing. You may be saying to yourself, "If I have to be dependent . . . if I have to surrender to someone . . . if I have to risk vulnerability, I don't want any of this fear thing. I'll just stay in control."

Too many of us, in our woundedness, equate vulnerability with *losing* control or failure. The reality is that choosing to *surrender* control and become exposed as someone in need creates opportunity for change, growth, and fulfillment.

The threat of failure is the voice of unhealthy, impaired fear. In its impaired state, fear says that we'll be found out as we really are—creatures of need who believe our needs won't be met or that neediness equals rejection.

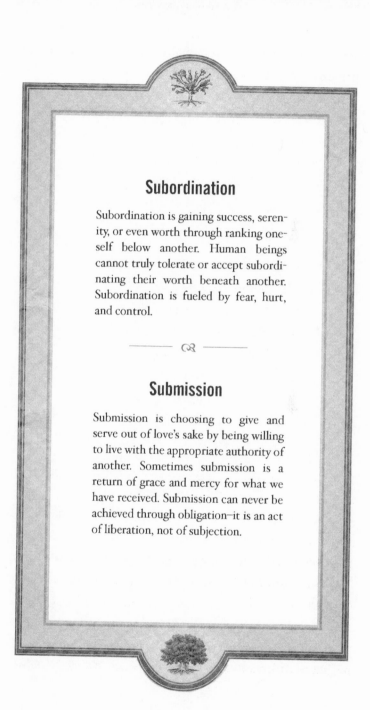

Subordination

Subordination is gaining success, serenity, or even worth through ranking oneself below another. Human beings cannot truly tolerate or accept subordinating their worth beneath another. Subordination is fueled by fear, hurt, and control.

———— ❧ ————

Submission

Submission is choosing to give and serve out of love's sake by being willing to live with the appropriate authority of another. Sometimes submission is a return of grace and mercy for what we have received. Submission can never be achieved through obligation—it is an act of liberation, not of subjection.

In these lies, we believe that our needs can't be met unless we do it by ourselves, which means denying and hiding our neediness. In an effort to mask our neediness, we grasp for control over things we don't have the ability to control. Instead of using fear to acknowledge the danger, evaluate the situation, and ask for help, we scramble in an attempt to control circumstances. The result is life lived in impaired fear—anxiety.

ANXIETY

Anxiety takes us away from what is true and makes us fretful, distrustful, impulsive, and controlling. In anxiety we rob ourselves of daily living and its experience. Instead, we try to control our future in order to prevent the recurrence of painful past experiences.

The solution of control over anxiety will inevitably increase anxiety because we cannot ever acquire enough control.

Anxiety as a solution to fear is self-sufficiency—the refusal to need openly and to face how we are made. We would rather be miserable or make others around us miserable than expose our feelings. We would rather enlist others to quell our anxiety than face our own heart's fears and our need for help.

The self-sufficiency we use to stop fear produces more anxiety because in order to control anxiety we focus on preventing rejection, humiliation, failure, not being acknowledged for our achievements, not performing to someone else's standard, not being loved, and all the things in our future we cannot touch. The solution of control over anxiety will inevitably increase anxiety because we cannot ever acquire enough control.

Fear manifested as anxiety is a physiological reaction that denies the heart and commands the brain to look externally to find a threat to explain our sense of dread. It is the fight-or-flight experience. If we are dealing with a true physical threat, fight or flight is necessary. The problem is that using fight or flight to address emotional and spiritual fears denies our hearts.

Anxiety misinforms us. It says for us to control when we need to let go.

For instance, the first time you tell someone that you love him or her, your heart throbs, your palms may sweat, your throat grows parched—you exhibit physical responses to something entirely emotional and spiritual. This physical response is the emotional and spiritual fear of the rejection of your vulnerability and neediness. It is a battle between fear and anxiety.

Anxiety commands that you make yourself invulnerable. Fear requests that you expose vulnerability and neediness to gain healthy control—the appropriate care of your own welfare.

VULNERABILITY

Any child will ask for help to go into the dark. We need to listen to this expression of need. Through his clear expression of vulnerability, a child can find comfort in the dark because of the hand that holds his tightly. The child who is forced to deny his heart, his true need for help exposed by fear, is left to run wildly through the dark, developing rituals to escape the fear of it or manufacture a multitude of excuses to avoid it.

Darkness isn't what the child fears so much. He fears being in the darkness alone. Vulnerability to need, once it has been rejected, becomes the object of fear. But in place of facing our fear through relationship, we grow anxious for control over our fears. Darkness then becomes the problem, when originally not having vulnerability honored was the real problem.

This short story of rejection of the heart becomes a long saga of survival. For too many of us, anxiety is an indication that we are trying to get away from having to deal with fear in our hearts by dreading something that has not happened, or trying to prevent the recurrence of something that has happened.

> We live in defensiveness against events that may or may not occur.
>
> We throw ourselves into the future and end up missing the present.
>
> We end up borrowing trouble.

Tragically, this solution often manufactures the very things we dread. For instance, if we dread being rejected and stay away from intimacy, we wind up alone—rejected. Our solutions for control become problems when we deeply and simply need to admit the truth: we are afraid.

RAGE

Another impaired expression of fear is rage. It results from refusing to face our fear of vulnerability. Rage lashes out

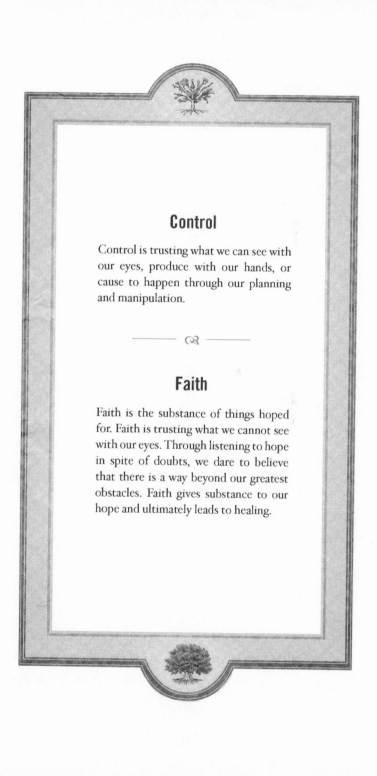

Control

Control is trusting what we can see with our eyes, produce with our hands, or cause to happen through our planning and manipulation.

———— ᘓ ————

Faith

Faith is the substance of things hoped for. Faith is trusting what we cannot see with our eyes. Through listening to hope in spite of doubts, we dare to believe that there is a way beyond our greatest obstacles. Faith gives substance to our hope and ultimately leads to healing.

silently or loudly to harm whatever is in its path—as numerous children, spouses, co-workers, and other innocents have tragically experienced.

Rage almost always lashes out from deep emotional and spiritual wounds. Rage-filled people are terrified of exposing their hearts. Rage, then, is a defense used against the heart to deny and hide our terror.

Rage destroys the benefit of fear because it denies the fact that fear even exists. Fear awakens us to potential emotional and spiritual harm. Rage tries to control the possibility of harm by rejecting fear and what the fear is telling us. Rage rejects our pain.

Rage is a physiological experience that defends against vulnerability by disconnecting or denying true fear. Rage says, "I'm helpless. I'm taking control of this situation right now. If you don't stop it, I'm going to kill you." The killing can be literal, but most often the killing occurs through threats of abandonment, punishment, "the silent treatment," verbal assaults, or myriad other things. Rage is effective only with people who love and need us; only loved ones will mistakenly tolerate this abusiveness.

Rage Versus Anger

Many of us mistakenly confuse rage and anger. We've been taught that anger and rage are the same thing. We've associated anger as a harmful, destructive force, when actually the harmful, destructive force occurs as a refusal to experience the fears of our hearts.

In truth, rage and anger are miles apart. Rage rejects the fear of having desire. Anger is an acknowledgment of the depth of our desire.

Rage denies our humanity with a willful fury against vulnerability. Anger acknowledges our humanity with all of its hungers.

Fear has in it a desire for something to stop, or a desire for something to start. In our anger we reach out in vulnerability, saying, "I want that to stop. I want this to change." We will know if we are fearful rather than full of rage by whether or not we can be in contact with other feelings and use those feelings for benefit.

Rage is a state of refusal. Anger is a state of openness and vulnerability.

By mistaking rage for anger, we end up thinking that someone else's anger is a rejection of us. Because we have experienced people raging at us, many of us have anxiety about anyone expressing anger toward us. When they raged at us, they were indeed rejecting us because they were harming us.

A Return to Fear and Full Life

To move from anxiety and rage back to healthy fear, we need to accept that we will experience hurt. This hurt, though, does not have to stop us from living out of the heart's desires in an open fashion. Even with hurt and the fear of hurt, we can through courage and healing continue to trust and believe that relationship is possible.

Many of us, as survivors, must also work through the past because hurt and the fear of heart pain have occurred so many times before that we believe more will just simply kill us. It is good to work through our fear because full life awaits us and the voice of the heart commands that we live fully as emotional and spiritual creatures. The first step is to admit that pain in our hearts exists, as well as the fear of exposing it. Healthy fear allows us to take that risk. Anxiety keeps us from taking any risk at all.

By acknowledging fear, we will eventually move away from anxiety and toward a deeper serenity found only in listening to the voice of the heart.

Fear tells us to go to our hearts and evaluate the experience. Anxiety demands that we look outside ourselves for answers when we need to look inside at our hearts.

We need to ask ourselves, "What do I fear? What am I afraid is going to happen?" By acknowledging fear, we will eventually move away from anxiety and toward a deeper serenity found only in listening to the voice of the heart.

The great benefit of fear is that it offers us the chance to face our human circumstances and tell the truth about them. We are vulnerable and in need. We grow in competence, interdependence, and trustworthiness through admission of vulnerability and neediness. Without fear there is no wisdom because we're not stopping to assess the circumstances, respect the challenges, reach out for help, prepare for the results, and then march into them.

THE GAIN OF FEAR

The more we gain wisdom, the more we are certain that healthy fear will lead us to beneficial circumstances.

> Healthy fear allows us to trust the authority (words, deeds, and hearts) of others and God.
>
> Healthy fear puts us in the position of greater influence and greater leadership.
>
> Healthy fear makes us wise because we can listen to the experience of life and preserve ourselves for good things.
>
> Healthy fear can allow us to accept serenity that comes only through God.
>
> Healthy fear gives us many benefits.

Fear is the beginning of wisdom. The recognition of our deep limitations that comes from admitted fear is the awakening of our need for God and others. This is not a mental acknowledgment; it is a heartfelt neediness.

As we discover our neediness, we find a God who is always in charge, in love, and on duty.

As our neediness is turned into dependence, the dependence is transformed into hope for good and trust that goodness is coming. As we allow ourselves to discover goodness, we also discover faith. This certainty eradicates anxiety.

Fear used well is the antidote to worry. Isn't that astounding?

Now in this knowledge of fear, go hug your children, kiss your father, tell your mother of your hurt, tell God you need more, tell your spouse you were wrong. Admit to your self your lack of sufficiency, your inability to control your circumstances, and your hunger for love. Release your anxieties, embrace your fears, and pursue wisdom. Grow into faith. Reach out for help. Give it away.

QUESTIONS FOR PERSONAL REFLECTION

1. What are the benefits of feeling fear? How has fear helped you?

2. What about trusting another person scares you?

3. Have you ever risked trusting someone even though you felt fear? If so, what happened? What did you feel as a result of risking that trust?

4. When has fear helped you take action and prepare for an event?

5. When are some times that you have been reactive, impulsive, or indecisive? What did you fear at those times?

6. When annoyances or worries strike, how do you deal with them? Do you ever try to force control in these situations? How do you go about it?

7. In what ways has fear helped you value yourself with good decisions?

Humble yourselves, therefore,
under God's mighty hand,
that he may lift you up in due time.
Cast all your anxiety on him
because he cares for you.

—1 Peter 5:6-7

CHAPTER 8

SHAME

ભ

S hame tells me: "I am limited." "I am mistake-ridden." "I have some answers, but I don't have all the answers." "I need you to help me; I can't do this alone." "We need each other."

Shame is the emotional and spiritual recognition of the potential to fail and to do harm, to succeed, and to love.

Shame elicits the experience of conscience and consciousness of our own limitation and giftedness. In the experience of shame, through realizing our gifts and limitations, we have empathy for others.

> We know and accept that we make mistakes so we can offer the same understanding to others.
>
> We know goodness and badness and help others recognize both.
>
> We also know and accept that we have gifts so we can offer others the same knowledge about themselves.

The empathy that is developed through shame illuminates the truth of our human condition. We become vulnerable to considering ourselves exactly as we are: feeling, needing, desiring, longing, hoping creatures who succeed and fail, who need daily, who desire great things even though we may fall short of finding them, who long for a fulfillment we cannot completely obtain, and who have abundant hope that some-day everything will be okay.

In seeing ourselves as we are, we find that we are full of dreams and capabilities, keepers of great worth who are also needy and unable a lot of the time to do what we say we're going to do or wish to do. We are glorious ruins in need of others and God.

HUMILITY

However, shame does not humiliate. It helps create humility within us. Humility grows out of the profound recognition of our limitations and of the capacities we possess in our giftedness. It helps us realize how incredibly fortunate we are to be who we are and at the same time, it shows us how deficient we are without others and God to help us live fully.

Most of us don't fully appreciate the value of our giftedness until we have been broken by circumstances in life.

You carry within yourself specific gifts that allow you to experience how wonderfully you are made. Discovering and experiencing these gifts will help you know your value in life (that you belong) and your ability to add to life (that you matter).

Most of us don't fully appreciate the value of our gift-edness until we have been broken by circumstances in life. In brokenness, we are offered the opportunity to see our powerlessness and neediness. These painful circumstances often break us of our pride-filled defiance against needing and break us of the fear that our lack of power will result in rejection.

Not until then do we acknowledge our gifts and stop using them only to prove ourselves. Only then do we start giving ourselves in service to others. In this sharing, we offer our gifts not because we *ought to* but because we *can't help doing so*. We are made to live out of the heart's expression of our giftedness.

We have all known someone like this. A teacher who has passion for her subject and her students, a pastor who loves to offer spiritual certainty and comfort to his congregation, a physician who genuinely cares for her patients, a mother who nurtures and cares beyond her own children and seems to adopt an entire neighborhood, or a father who coaches a baseball team long after his children have grown up. These individuals offer themselves because they cannot help doing so. They have found that the greatest fulfillment in life is to be of maximum service through their giftedness. These same persons are also amazed at times that they get to give so much.

LIVING IN GIFTEDNESS

Living in our giftedness is a form of expressing who we are. When we actually live as who we are, three things happen:

1. We delight in God's creation.
2. We are humbled that God made us like we are (gifted and limited).
3. We are unable to ignore the desire to give ourselves to something greater.

In delight we find joy. In humility we are grateful and merciful. Being unable to ignore our desire to serve can be tremendously painful; until we let ourselves pursue that desire, we will feel emotional and spiritual pain. Yet in the pursuit of that desire we are willing to go through great pain in order to have our desire fulfilled.

Living with healthy shame is living within your appropriate authority. It is living how God has made you—specifically using your gifts and talents in maximum service to others while also recognizing the limitations of your gifts and seeking the giftedness of others and their appropriate authority. In so doing, you are involved in the authentic pursuit of living fully, responding appropriately out of your spiritual and emotional gifts. These gifts involve physical talents and/or intellectual acumen, but they are submitted to the primacy of the heart's voice.

For example, a laborer produces using his hands, but is not necessarily present in mind and heart. A craftsman uses his hands and mind to build, but may not be moved by his heart. An artist is present in both body and mind, but uses these as tools to create from his heart or even from emotional and spiritual desires. We all fall into one of these three categories, whether we are a harpist, pastor, physician, or welder. Even the "lowliest" work is full if the artist is present. The artist starts not with a canvas, but with desire. When we live humbly from our hearts, open to our gifts and willing to see our limitations, we cannot help but have influence in an appropriate, authentic way.

The humility that occurs when we live out of our gifts and limitations leads us to the awareness of our appropriate

Self-centeredness

Self-centeredness is a form of egocentrism. It is a focused concern on our appearance, achievements, good works, and self-will while disregarding the true well-being of others. The ego-centered person's focus is, "How am I doing?" He or she looks for answers through comparison and competition. Our society's overconcern with self-esteem promotes a culture of egocentrism.

———— ⚭ ————

Self-awareness

Self-awareness is a struggle to identify, expose, and express who we are, even when that discovery hurts or points to a need for change. By looking within and listening to others, the self-aware person has answers to the questions "Who am I?" "What do I believe?" "Why am I doing this?" Because self-awareness is usually preceded by brokenness, self-awareness creates a sense of deep gratitude.

place—on a team, in a corporation, in the universe. Therefore, shame is the feeling that allows us to move into cooperation and community, because it says, "I have my talents; I also have my limitations, and so do you. I'll share what I have, as will you, and that way you and I can create something beautiful and true." The greatest achievements happen through this kind of cooperation rather than through competition.

A CONSCIOUSNESS OF INCOMPLETENESS

Shame is the feeling that first brings us into relationship with ourselves because it makes us conscious of our incompleteness. Even in our confidence and ability, shame helps us see that we need others. It points out our shortcomings, our humanity, so that we better understand ourselves for who we uniquely are, so that we can value ourselves for how we were uniquely created. Despite all our shortcomings, we are quite capable and competent—sometimes even extraordinary.

In this consciousness of gifts and shortcomings, we recognize our capacity to fall short of our desires and dreams, but we don't stop dreaming.

Another gift of shame is that it keeps us from worshiping ourselves and our giftedness. We recognize our gifts and are grateful for them. We remember that we are more than our gifts and that we will never escape our natural inferiority: "I'm not a king or queen. I'm royal but fulfilled only as a servant."

Shame tells us that we will always be people who are capable of harming others and failing. No matter how much we wish to be loving, good, kind, and talented, we will continue to fall short of pure desires. We will always need help.

While shame tells me about myself, this self-recognition also tells me about others. This sensitivity to empathy is called conscience. It lets me know that I don't have all the answers, and neither do you. It says, "I'm not God, but neither are you. Let's help each other."

In knowing that I have pain, I can recognize and accept your pain. I can say, "I feel hurt inside to see you in such pain."

In this consciousness of gifts and shortcomings, we recognize our capacity to fall short of our desires and dreams, but we don't stop dreaming.

Therefore, through shame, I can be in true relationship with you because ours is not a relationship based solely upon our individual abilities or what we can offer each other, but it is a relationship grounded in our commonality as part of humanity.

TOXIC SHAME

Whereas shame leads to self-acceptance in relationship with ourselves, others, and God, impaired shame creates self-rejection. In impaired shame we have learned to equate humility with humiliation, failure with uselessness, and inability with worthlessness. This experience makes healthy shame toxic. Our shame has become so distorted that it is unrecognizable as a help for relationship.

Rather than lead us to acknowledge our neediness, toxic shame entangles our hearts, tightly binding them up, leaving us unable to experience full life because we can't experience our natural place. We believe we should hide who we are, and we center our lives on doing it.

This toxic shame is really rejection of the image of God we all carry in our hearts. Toxic shame denies our humanity as feeling, needing, desiring, longing, and hoping creatures. We reject our hearts through the belief that the way we are made is defective.

Toxic shame denies our humanity as feeling, needing, desiring, longing, and hoping creatures.

Impaired shame comes from our pasts. We have learned for survival's sake to hide, reject, or minimize our hearts. If significant people whom we love insist or need for us to deny our heart's content, they poison us with toxic shame. Those who are capable of teaching us self-rejection are almost always people we love. Everyone I have ever met who has this impaired state of shame received it from those who had power over his or her heart.

Toxic shame helps us so deny our natural condition that we are left with anxiety (dread of what will happen) and a demand to control (struggle to keep others away from our hearts). In healthy shame we say, "I am limited," which leads us to ask for help. In toxic shame, "I am limited" becomes "I am a mistake." This poisons the truth of our hearts and forces us to "go it alone."

In toxic shame, we reject our natural call to seek help,

reach for others, and expose our true giftedness and creativity. In fact, we use our gifts not to express ourselves, but to become persons of value based upon performance. Toxic shame tells us that if we show our true selves, we will be rejected.

Those who feel toxic shame are very hard on themselves. They are always trying to earn everything—from love to grace. They live with a millstone around their necks. To hide this pain, many shame-bound people spend their lives achieving and obtaining great things, but never experience the wholeness for which they were working.

SHAMELESSNESS

Even farther removed from healthy shame is its impaired expression in shamelessness. Denying their natural createdness and rejecting all humility, shameless people act as if they are incapable of being at fault (narcissists) or as if only they are allowed responsibility for problems (martyrs). Shameless people behave in grandiose ways.

Shameless people instill toxic shame in those who love them and are vulnerable to them. Parents, coaches, teachers, pastors, physicians, and others have great responsibility to live lives of healthy shame, seeking forgiveness for shameless behavior. These same people have great responsibility also for breaking the bondage of toxic shame, which demeans the marvelous beauty of how God made us.

THE GAIN OF SHAME

Healthy shame is an admission of the truth, awakening vulnerability in your limitations and competency in your giftedness. The gain of healthy shame is that it helps you live in intimacy with yourself, others, and God through the development of humility.

Feeling shame allows you to recognize the commonality among all people, accept differences, and accept your own limitations.

In this humility, you recognize that life is a journey of progress, not perfection.

Healthy shame helps you recognize that in your humility, you can offer mercy and forgiveness because you are as capable as anyone of being wrong and causing pain.

And healthy shame prepares you to accept love as a gift, and become loving as a result.

QUESTIONS FOR PERSONAL REFLECTION

1. Have life's pain and problems ever humbled you in a way that you see as beneficial? If so, how? What do you feel about these experiences now?

2. What experiences and circumstances in your life have caused you to experience brokenness? Have these events caused you to reach out for help? If so, to whom did you reach? If not, what stopped you?

3. What was a time when you reached out in mercy and empathy to another because you recognized yourself in that person's pain?

4. How can healthy shame help clarify and illuminate your conscience?

5. Do you equate needing others and God with being weak? Explain.

6. What do you feel about being a needy, dependent creature?

7. On whom or what do you depend most when difficulties arise?

8. What keeps you from reaching out for help?

9. Has healthy shame allowed you to reach out for God and find that God is doing for you what you cannot do? If so, when? If not, what do you feel about this possibility?

"Come to me, all who are weary and burdened, and I will give you rest. Take my yoke upon you and learn from me, for I am gentle and humble in heart, and you will find rest for your souls. For my yoke is easy and my burden is light."

—Matthew 11:28-30

CHAPTER 9

GUILT

CR

Guilt is good. Guilt brings freedom. It is the emotional and spiritual gift that allows us to feel and accept that we've done something wrong. It sparks the wish and vulnerability for change. It prompts us to seek forgiveness. And forgiveness sets us free. Guilt is all about forgiveness, if we want freedom.

Through feeling shame, we know ourselves with humility (consciousness), and we know that we are capable of both wonderful and terrible actions (conscience). Shame is the feeling that recognizes our limitations and our capability to do harm.

Guilt is what we feel when we actually *do* something wrong. Guilt follows shame, for in our humility we know that we can do things that are wrong, fall short, wound others, fail our personal value system and standards, and cause regret upon regret.

Consciousness and conscience help me feel shame and know my value system because I can see and experience pain in myself and others. Beyond shame, guilt tells me that I have broken the guidelines, especially the ones that harm me and others—I have done wrong.

BEHAVIOR TOWARD OTHERS

Guilt is always about behavior (planned or acted) toward another. It tells us there is something in the heart that we're not seeing or owning up to. Behavior and plans are indications of the state of the heart. We feel guilty about what we do, yet our behaviors often indicate that something is going on inside our hearts that we're refusing to acknowledge, address, respond to, or accept. Through guilt, the heart confronts behavior, and behavior, in turn, exposes the state of our hearts.

Through guilt, the heart confronts behavior, and behavior, in turn, exposes the state of our hearts.

For example, a person who behaves sarcastically may be refusing to address suppressed anger or hurt. Or a person who is having an affair may be refusing to acknowledge loneliness and hurt that have become apathy and resentment in the marriage.

Although guilt is never about the worth of a person, it certainly can be a voice of confrontation about the condition of that person's heart, whether healthy or impaired. It offers the opportunity to face truth and change.

When I look into the face of my wife knowing that I have said something that scorched her heart, I can see her pain, feel my guilt, and take responsibility for what I have done, regardless of the "big explanation" about my behavior. When I recognize her pain, I also see and understand the depth of harm that I can do, and this harm is against the one I am committed to desire and nurture as a sacred trust.

In her face I see the hurt, and in her voice I hear the woundedness. I see my need for change and—but for pride or toxic shame—want it badly. By listening to the voice of my heart, I become vulnerable to forgiveness and my desire to change. It is through vulnerability to others and desiring to change that relationship can be reconciled, even restored.

THE WILLINGNESS TO BE HUMBLE

The amount of forgiveness I receive is directly related to my willingness to be fully truthful, exposed, and surrendered—that is, humbled (healthy shame). This is what makes guilt so painful and forgiveness so terrifying.

In guilt, I am offering and exposing my heart in humility to another. I am exposing my heart and the harms I have caused others and God. I am asking for a decision about the future of that relationship from the person I have harmed.

Whenever we genuinely seek forgiveness, we are free, whether the others forgive us or not.

In feeling guilt and seeking forgiveness with others, we experience one of two things—either we receive forgiveness, or we don't. When we go to someone we have harmed and expose our hearts in guilt, they will offer us forgiveness then or over time, or they will maintain distrust and resentment in their inability or unwillingness to forgive. In either instance, if we are truthful and vulnerable in seeking forgiveness, then we will be free of the pain of guilt because in honestly seeking forgiveness we exposed our hearts for relationship. In both situations, our hearts are given back to us, one in reconciliation and freedom, the other in sadness, hope, and freedom. The decision the others make is whether or not to honor our hearts. Whenever we genuinely seek forgiveness, we are free, whether the others forgive us or not.

Conversely, if we still feel guilt after we have sought forgiveness, we need to listen to our hearts carefully to know what we are still hiding and what we still need forgiveness for. If the sense of guilt persists after honest searching, it's probably not guilt. It is usually toxic shame telling us that we are bad, defective, incompetent, or unforgivable.

Unlike guilt that gives us freedom, toxic shame increases the bondage of hopelessness. It tells us that we are never free. It always tries to work for forgiveness—to make us perfect. It tries to make us earn what is a gift from another's heart.

Guilt always points to the need for forgiveness and change—the need to be reconciled with our own hearts, with others, and with God. Therefore, guilt is relational. It is the voice of the heart speaking to the pain we have caused ourselves, others, and God. We desire to be in sincere, authentic relationships with others and God. Guilt and the healthy directions it can take lead us to fulfill that desire.

THE MYTH OF SELF-FORGIVENESS

Ironically, our society has taught us that we can forgive ourselves. Our culture commands, in fact, that we be so "okay" with ourselves that we have become insulated from guilt and its connection to the heart. Self-esteem is protected from the painful recognition of harmful actions. These actions, we believe, can be fixed somehow with goodwill or sufficiency.

Reaction

Reaction is an unexamined and unplanned behavior based upon the actions of another. It suggests a lack of awareness of our hearts. It reveals how we see ourselves as victims of other people's power. Reaction makes others the "masters" of our lives. Reaction is having our needs only partially met while keeping our hearts hidden.

———— ❧ ————

Response

Response considers the heart's truths and is based upon emotional and spiritual examination. It never attempts to control or shame another, or hide heart truths. Because responsive people know their hearts, they can act in truth and clarity when life's difficulties surface.

The idea that I can forgive myself is a delusion of grandiosity and arrogance that damages all of my heart's hunger for intimacy. Forgiving myself makes me a god. This delusional belief screams arrogance because it is an attempt to become a god through my own self-sufficiency. There is no such thing as someone forgiving oneself.

Without guilt we miss the beauty of being loved.

I can only be forgiven by another or by God. I can't crawl up into my lap and say, "Chip, I'm sorry I did this to me." However, I can acknowledge that I treat myself terribly and irresponsibly, and that I need to ask God and others to forgive me and help me.

When I attempt to forgive myself, I am really in need of no one. I am denying my need of others or God to do for me what I cannot do.

When I try to forgive myself, I'm actually attempting to make me feel better about what I did to repair the temporary damage to my self-esteem. Self-forgiveness is a form of tricking oneself into believing that justifying, rationalizing, or excusing intentions is the same as forgiveness. Forgiveness is about me needing your help or God's help, not my own solutions.

We don't create ourselves; we are created. We don't forgive ourselves; we are forgiven. We are not God; we need God and the help of others.

In fact, the only real power we have is the ability to refuse the One who owns us, made us, and pursues our hearts—

to refuse the truth within our hearts. When we attempt to forgive ourselves, we reject that we are image bearers of God, and we refuse our dependency upon God and others.

To refuse our need of forgiveness or to believe that all can be made well by good intentions and hard work is to reject mercy and grace. Mercy brings tenderness to our lives. Grace brings amazement. Both bring gratefulness. Without guilt we miss the beauty of being loved.

PASSING THE BUCK

So the questions to ask yourself are:

- "Am I willing to feel guilt?"
- "Am I willing to listen to my heart and lay claim to my harmful intentions and actions?"
- "Am I able to go to another and God and expose those intentions and actions in truth and vulnerability?"

If you're not, you are not concerned with forgiveness as much as you're concerned with justification and explanation.

Would you rather be forgiven or justified? Do you really seek to be forgiven and rebuild trust, or do you offer explanation as to why you did what you did so that others won't have feelings about your behavior?

Would you like to be given freedom through forgiveness, or would you rather be justified in your harm of another? If you are seeking justification, you are really trying to find a way of not taking responsibility. If you do so, then you will blame the other person through your explanation. It sounds something like this: "If you had not _____, then I would not have _____."

Intimate relationships of all kinds are marked by each person's willingness to seek forgiveness, which begins with feeling guilt. Impaired relationships are characterized by the way in which members provide explanation or blame to avoid the feeling of guilt and the need for admission and forgiveness.

If we don't seek forgiveness, then we are on some level trying to make ourselves okay or others okay with our harming them or being harmed by them. This excuse making keeps us away from our hearts and, therefore, blocks intimacy.

Until we stop offering excuses and start asking for forgiveness, the broken record that says, "They did the best they could," will continue to play, attempting to justify without seeking reconciliation. We make ourselves temporarily feel good with these statements, but we avoid the heart's pain and heart solutions with them.

In turn, we offer such explanations to our children or students or parishioners or patients. They will then pass them on to theirs. The end result is that no one finds the intimacy they are seeking because no one tells the truth about the state of their hearts. What needs to be accepted is that we did not do the "best" we could. We are all in need of forgiveness.

BLAME

Another way we avoid feeling guilt is by hanging on to blame. Blame becomes a wall between our hearts and our actions as a way to evade our humanity.

Blame judges the ones we believe have harmed us so that we don't have to feel our own hurt and often the heart's desire for restoration of relationship. We judge others as being unwilling, bad, or in denial so that we do not have to make our own hearts vulnerable to the ones who harmed us.

Through blame, we justify behaving like the people

that we believe have harmed us, giving us the "right" to be hard-hearted or distant "because of them." Blame helps avoid the guilt of refusing our own desire for restoration or reconciliation.

Both rationalization and blame keep our hearts numb to the pain of guilt and closed off from our desire for intimacy. We escape from the pain of guilt by not taking ownership for what we do. We claim that our harmful actions are justified; therefore, we don't have to need others or God.

Intimate relationships of all kinds are marked by each person's willingness to seek forgiveness, which begins with feeling guilt.

The impaired expression of guilt, then, is pride. Pride is a form of shamelessness—a defiance that rejects our condition. It denies the heart's hunger for relationship with others, especially God, because pride won't allow us to need help, others, or forgiveness. It also won't allow us to find forgiveness because in our pride we hide our hurt from others.

As another expression of impaired guilt, toxic shame is the reverse of pride. Toxic shame and pride block us from the freedom that guilt can offer.

Pride says, "I don't need it." Toxic shame says, "I will never deserve it." Pride works forever to maintain the right to need no one. Toxic shame works to earn the right (worth) to be intimate with someone.

Each impaired expression of guilt is an attempt to earn love and worth or have no need of it at all.

THE GAIN OF GUILT

Guilt is our most precious emotional and spiritual gift from God. Accompanied by healthy shame, guilt propels us to transparently turn ourselves over to the care of others and ultimately God in order to find forgiveness and freedom. This relinquishing of the heart to another has transforming power—the power to unite us more closely in relationship with others where harm once kept us apart. The deeper the harm before forgiveness, the deeper the relationship can be when forgiveness is granted.

The deeper the harm before forgiveness, the deeper the relationship can be when forgiveness is granted.

You see, paradoxically, it is with those you have harmed, sought forgiveness from, and received forgiveness from that you are able to have the most fulfilling relationships. It is by truthfully revealing your heart to others and God that you find full life and healing from the pain of old wounds that are infected with unresolved guilt. You also find love as a gift of grace that you receive through admission, not merit.

Forgiveness is imperative for abundant living. You need to go to the people you have harmed and ask for forgiveness. Where you need forgiveness that cannot be offered by another person, you need to reveal truthfully your guilt to God, offering your heart in the trust that God will provide forgiveness in return. In this way, your heart finds rest and freedom from the burden of living under the weight of guilt.

QUESTIONS FOR PERSONAL REFLECTION

1. Remember of a time when you sought forgiveness from another. What was most difficult about that experience? How did that experience affect your relationship with that person?

2. How can acknowledging your guilt bring you freedom?

3. What were some times when others told you that they felt hurt by your actions? How did you respond? Did you deny or justify your actions in order to minimize your guilt? Did you try to turn the tables? Did you ask for forgiveness? How are those relationships today?

4. How is your guilt truly only about your behavior (planned or acted)?

5. Who have you harmed lately? Have you asked for forgiveness? If not, what stopped you?

6. Many people associate guilt with worthlessness. Have you ever done this? How can this behavior inhibit your relationships? How can guilt be beneficial to you?

Then young women will dance and be glad,
young men and old as well.
I will turn their mourning into gladness;
I will give them comfort and joy
instead of sorrow.

—Jeremiah 31:13

CHAPTER 10

GLAD

☞

I remember asking my wife about the pain and joy of being pregnant and giving birth to our sons. I wanted to know about her gladness in it all. She said that gladness was a part of all the hope in being pregnant, even in the pain. But the joy was fullest when she held each son in her arms for the first time. She found gladness in her hopes and anticipations, but more gladness came with hope's fulfillment.

Wherever there is hope, there is gladness. Wherever hope is fulfilled, there is more gladness.

Gladness comes to those who know and persistently pursue their hearts' desires. To find gladness, we need to be vulnerable to our hearts' intentions and pursue desires that we know in our hearts to be true, noble, right, pure, lovely, admirable, or excellent. Knowing our hearts' intentions and desires requires feeling fully, for every feeling identifies our needs and illuminates our desires.

Gladness, then, is a result of our willingness to feel the other seven feelings.

Hurt speaks to our desire for healing and wholeness.

Loneliness speaks to our desire for relationship.

Sadness speaks to our desire to honor and value what matters to our hearts.

Anger speaks to our desire to risk and accept pain in order to achieve.

Fear speaks to our desire to be prepared, choose wisely, and succeed.

Shame speaks to our desire to have abundant life in the understanding of our limitations and to serve something greater than ourselves.

Guilt speaks to our desire to be reconciled and unburdened so we can live in the freedom of forgiveness.

Gladness comes as a result of our willingness to experience our whole hearts in successes or failures. Gladness speaks to the gratification of having our desires fulfilled, and even to our willingness to have desire itself.

GLADNESS VERSUS HAPPINESS

Gladness is not about being happy or getting what we want. The word *happiness* finds its origins based in the word *happenstance*, which means that circumstances dictate our sense of well-being or serenity. Happiness controls externally.

Gladness is about desiring deeply and having a willingness to walk through pain in the pursuit of the desire.

Gladness is about desiring deeply and having a willingness to walk through pain in the pursuit of the desire. The outcome of the desire doesn't matter as much as living in the heart openly and truthfully. You see, gladness is found in waiting for the fulfillment of desires and believing that fulfillment is possible. In risking desire, we are hoping for gladness to be fulfilled. But even if the desire is not realized, the hope will be and gladness will be experienced.

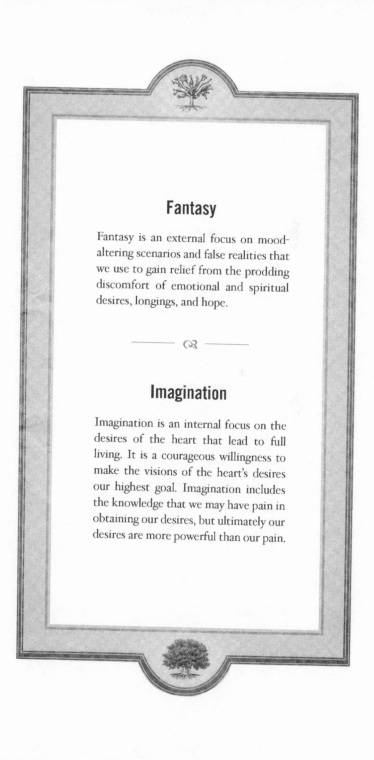

Fantasy

Fantasy is an external focus on mood-altering scenarios and false realities that we use to gain relief from the prodding discomfort of emotional and spiritual desires, longings, and hope.

Imagination

Imagination is an internal focus on the desires of the heart that lead to full living. It is a courageous willingness to make the visions of the heart's desires our highest goal. Imagination includes the knowledge that we may have pain in obtaining our desires, but ultimately our desires are more powerful than our pain.

To hope is to live from our hearts, and in living out of our hearts we find fulfillment. As frightening as it may seem, gladness is not about outcomes. It's about living fully. Sometimes even our hopes are dashed and we're left feeling sadness and hurt.

My sister deeply loved a man from the moment they met, but it wasn't until twenty years later that they were married. Six months after their wedding, he died. Her dreams and desires for them evaporated like a mist. Today, after walking through her deep grief, she would not trade those six months for anything. Of course she would choose him over the grief. But in her desire to love and be loved she found fulfillment in her willingness to live from her heart. She found gladness as she walked through the other feelings.

Living life on life's terms is the realization that much, if not most, of life and its joys occur around pain and loss.

True gladness comes as a gift of living our lives to the fullest, but it is with pain that we receive the gift. While everyone fantasizes about heart gladness, not everyone is willing to risk obtaining it because it comes through the risk of getting hurt and of not being in control. In this way gladness takes great risk, courage, vulnerability, and trust.

Gladness, then, is born out of brokenness and pain— brokenness of self-sufficiency, self-protection, and self-will and the pain of waiting and not having desires realized. Brokenness and pain bring us to the gifts that can come from admission and surrender to our vulnerability, neediness, and dependence. Alone, we are not enough and we never will be.

FACING LIFE ON LIFE'S TERMS

Gladness can occur only as we face life on life's terms. It requires us to honestly struggle and accept that life is chock-full of mystery, revelations, joy, confusion, elation, tragic losses, powerful reunions, restorations, divisions, passions, and pains. Living life on life's terms also requires us to recognize that we have very little control over it.

When the walls around our hearts are broken down, we are set free to experience and choose full living. We are needy, dependent creatures who need to surrender our hearts so that we can experience how we are made—to be in relationship with ourselves, others, and especially God. When we do this daily, we begin to experience life through the heart and we begin to experience the heart of God. We recognize that while life is often depressing, frustrating, and frightening, it is also wonderful, magnificent, and glorious.

Living life on life's terms is the realization that much, if not most, of life and its joys occur around pain and loss. Living life on life's terms allows us to face the fact that we aren't in control and that our dreams may never come true, and, even if they do, we will keep moving past them once we obtain them.

By living life on life's terms, we develop much more wisdom and ability to feel the other seven feelings. These feelings are made for life's fulfillment in relationship, which brings joy.

We are sorely mistaken and misguided if we use the gift of feelings as permission to be pessimistic, hopeless, doubtful, antagonistic, resentful, self-pitying, or unfulfilled. But if, in all of the warp and woof of living, we dare allow our hearts to be completely involved, we will find renewed acceptance and clearer understanding of life.

In this acceptance and understanding comes joy. But again, joy comes through the willingness to feel pain as we pursue living. We risk living with the potential of pain, or we give up a fulfilling life by committing our lives to survival through self-protection.

When a father gives his daughter away in marriage, it is a painful experience. He has sadness about knowing that their relationship has changed again—she has grown up and is leaving. He fears whether she will be okay as he lets go again. His heart hurts in knowing that he can't retrace steps and correct mistakes beyond saying, "I'm sorry."

Joy comes through his tears in knowing that her heart's desires are being realized, and he gets to be present to see it all take place. Because his heart is completely involved, his pain helps him appreciate the fullness of his life and increases his joy and almost certainly increases his daughter's joy too.

No one reaches the highest peaks of life unless she is willing to fall to the greatest depths. No one can experience deep, heartfelt joy unless he is able and willing to grieve to the core, even having hopes disappointed by not being fulfilled. Gladness, therefore, is only for the courageous because it requires risking emotional and spiritual pain in the midst of living lives as we are made to live them—fully in relationship.

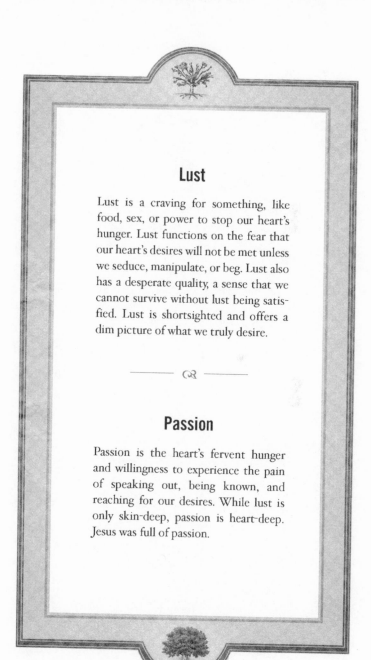

Lust

Lust is a craving for something, like food, sex, or power to stop our heart's hunger. Lust functions on the fear that our heart's desires will not be met unless we seduce, manipulate, or beg. Lust also has a desperate quality, a sense that we cannot survive without lust being satisfied. Lust is shortsighted and offers a dim picture of what we truly desire.

Passion

Passion is the heart's fervent hunger and willingness to experience the pain of speaking out, being known, and reaching for our desires. While lust is only skin-deep, passion is heart-deep. Jesus was full of passion.

HAPPINESS

Because gladness is so risky, the moment that many of us begin to experience it, we want to hold it and use it as a prevention against pain. It feels so good that we wish to capture it, make it our own, and take control of it so that we can keep the experience instead of recognizing it as a gift of full living.

Controlling gladness requires that we try to manufacture it in an effort to make ourselves *happier*. We turn this pure internal experience into an experience that is detached from the heart. We are trying to force our hearts into joy, much like demanding that a bride or groom be joyful in an arranged marriage. When we do this, we are usually running from the fear of dealing with the heart's pains.

When we attempt to manufacture gladness, we are trying to snatch from the external world something that will make safe or satiate the internal life. The attempt to manufacture emotional and spiritual fulfillment is an attempt to avoid dealing truthfully with the heart.

Instead of listening to the heart and moving into relationship, we offer the heart a fix. The fix is meant to control the heart by numbing any feeling we wish to escape. By numbing the feelings, we also are shutting down our needs, desires, longings, and hope.

Fixes are our attempts to stop our dependence upon others and God for life fulfillment. Happiness allows our hearts to be controlled by external circumstances. These external circumstances make us slaves to the current situation or, at the very least, temporary masters over them. Hypervigilance becomes our watchword, and restlessness or bondage becomes the result.

SENSUOUS PLEASURE

When the heart is numbed, gladness can only be experienced in sensuous ways. Sensuous pleasure is indeed real pleasure, but it is a very temporary substitute for how much the heart can offer us if we have courage. Pleasure that is detached from our hearts is only skin deep.

**When our hearts aren't present,
we attempt to make ourselves happy
through the brain, skin, or self-will.**

When our hearts aren't present, we attempt to make ourselves happy through the brain, skin, or self-will. We use the brain to find adrenaline or meaning. We use the skin to "feel good" by experiencing physical pleasure. Or we use willpower as the fuel to fix ourselves or achieve worth as surrogate fulfillment.

For example, we plan activity upon activity in an effort to distract our hearts so that we don't have to listen to them. Or we organize our lives around what will entertain us, distracting ourselves with diversions such as running, sex, overeating, or going to the spa. Or we experience worth only at work, where we can perform and produce and gain recognition through our success.

Impaired gladness, then, is a form of intellectual, physical, or counterfeit emotional gratification that is an illegitimate attempt to do something legitimate. This "gratification" is used to create mental stimulation, physical pleasures, or emotional thrills that may temporarily meet our needs, but miss the truth about us as spiritual beings. Satisfaction is a poor substitute for gratification.

We legitimately need to hear our emotional and spiritual hungers that the heart voices through feelings, but we need to answer those hungers with legitimate means. Counterfeit fulfillment temporarily satisfies, but it misses the truth about us as spiritual beings.

For example, how many times have you been to an event that you've really anticipated and looked forward to? "It's going be so great. It's going to feel so good." You wait until then to feel—to live. Then, when you finally get in the midst of that great situation, you recognize the lack of gladness or gratification. Satisfaction cannot sustain the heart.

Manufactured Joy

Where is it? It was never there to begin with. This attempt to manufacture joy of the heart through external means is not the answer to the heart's questions.

In manufacturing gladness, many of us live vicariously. We will sit on our bottoms in a theater while life flows over us instead of getting up and going out and living it, getting sweaty and dirty in life. Movies may teach us truths of the heart, but they are not living.

Is it okay to go to movies because you're just tired and want to escape for a while or because you simply like the entertainment? Yes, of course.

If you intentionally know you're doing it, take ownership of that. Acknowledge that you need rest or desire to be entertained. Know what it cannot give.

When you go to that movie, are you taking ownership,

Satisfaction

Satisfaction comes from satiation—the attempt to find comfort by avoiding the heart's necessary pain. We use sensual means to silence the heart's desires, ultimately leaving us lusting for more. We satiate our brains, our stomachs, our genitals, and our actions with a focus on avoidance. We avoid our senses (feelings) by converting them to the sensual.

Gratification

Gratification comes from gratitude. It uses the pleasure and passion we have for life that comes from being adept at feelings. Feelings allow us to live fully in the vulnerability of relationship with ourselves, God, and others. Gratification operates out of our God-given craving for life and allows us to press into a future with a passion in the midst of pain.

or are you just sort of sneaking off, hoping to get stimulated, titillated, or intoxicated by what you see?

The impaired experience of gladness is entertainment—satisfaction of sensuality rather than gratification of sensitivity. Entertainment is wonderful—dancing, concerts, movies, ball games, trout fishing—but if you are not consuming the emotional and spiritual food of relationship, you cannot gratify what you're created to have fulfilled.

We legitimately need to hear our emotional and spiritual hungers that the heart voices through feelings, but we need to answer those hungers with legitimate means.

I am not condemning ball games. Enjoy them; but they're not going to be more than they are.

You will not reach the mountaintop of life at a football game. Trying to do so is a refusal to acknowledge the state of your heart and the true hungers within you. Movies are great and ball games are great, but there's a whole lot more to life.

Instead of going into our hearts and experiencing the vulnerability of feelings so that we awaken to how we are made, too many of us attempt to live our lives without focusing on our hearts. Such a life may temporarily satiate our sensual expectations, but it cannot gratify our deep heart hungers. We hunger to be in real relationship.

Saying, "I'm sorry," to someone you've harmed can be much more fulfilling and joyful than spending two hours at a movie that you have waited two months to see.

THE GAIN OF GLADNESS

Gladness is a derivative of admitting and surrendering to the fact that we are powerless, and that God is doing for us what we cannot do.

- "I've found that I'm not in charge."
- "I can let go."
- "I know that God is here and in control, wherever I am."

That feels good. That is fulfillment. That is gladness.

When we talk about gladness, we are really talking about brokenness and the fulfillment that comes from brokenness. Fulfilled of heart or "blessed" are the "poor in spirit" because they will become people who face the depth of their hunger to live fully as emotional and spiritual creatures. Those who have found lasting gladness have faced life on life's terms and have still held on to their hearts. Without first knowing brokenness, every other pleasure we achieve or manufacture is an attempt to escape our fundamental neediness.

Our hearts are touched only if they are vulnerable to being fully seen and fully known.

Ultimately, gladness comes as a distinctive characteristic of someone who has surrendered his heart to something or someone greater than himself. Ultimate fulfillment in life—gladness—is a matter of the heart, and at the heart's deepest core we are truly fulfilled by a consuming relationship with God.

By facing that we are emotional and spiritual creatures

created to live fully in relationship with ourselves, others, and God, we also face that our greatest joy is in being who God made us to be. Our hearts are touched only if they are vulnerable to being fully seen and fully known.

Through the breaking of the walls around your heart, which is painful, you find the gift of fulfillment. When you give your heart to real relationship, you discover the joys of true closeness, acceptance, dependency, trust, risk, giving, and love. You live.

QUESTIONS FOR PERSONAL REFLECTION

1. What is the difference between "being happy" and feeling gladness or joy?

2. In what ways do you attempt to manufacture gladness? How do you try to escape from the difficulty and pain of life?

3. Do you try to make those whom you love happy? If so, in what ways? How is this behavior harmful to relationships?

4. How do you celebrate yourself or others being alive?

5. How do you express your joy to others and God?

6. How is your emotional and spiritual pain an intricate part of your emotional and spiritual joy?

7. Have you ever experienced joy in the midst of a painful experience? If so, describe it? If not, in what ways did you defend your heart from the pain?

8. Is the joy of love, the celebration of being fully alive in relationship, worth the pain?

Taste and see that the LORD is good;
blessed is the man who takes refuge in him.

—Psalm 34:8

The LORD is close to the brokenhearted
and saves those who are crushed in spirit.

—Psalm 34:18

CONCLUSION

⊗

After reading an early manuscript for this book, a friend said, "So, I'm a bird in a nest and I don't have wings. What's the solution?" He wanted to know what to do with the voice of his heart after he recognized how his heart spoke. He had discovered that he is indeed an emotional and spiritual creature in need of living fully in relationship with himself, with others, and with God.

The solution is to live fully. But the beginning of the solution he was looking for is to recognize and feel his feelings, tell the truth about his heart to those who are trustworthy, and give the truth of his heart to God, then allow God to do what God does. Simply put, if we do these three things—feel our feelings, tell the truth, and give it to God—full life will follow. The process of life, God created.

Feeling our feelings is about beginning to take responsibility for the content of our hearts. It requires us to live out of how our hearts are made and use our feelings to experience and add to relationships—first with ourselves, then with others.

By knowing my heart, I discover my hunger for life and my inability to heal or fulfill myself alone. This recognition of powerlessness and vulnerability begins to genuinely awaken me to my need for others and God.

Telling the truth about my heart means that I reveal to others the authentic, unvarnished experience of my self. This experience is never a reason to be honest with others in order to harm them. The truth focuses on me and my vulnerabilities—my feelings, needs, desires, longings, and hope.

If we are truthful, really truthful, about our hearts in relationship with ourselves, others, and God, we will discover newfound intimacy. This experience is hard but rich work. Telling the truth challenges us to go to others and God in our neediness. By feeling our feelings and telling the truth, we are confronted with our limitations and our incompleteness.

This is where my friend was, as he said, like a bird in a nest without wings. He recognized his desire to fly—his hunger for more life. The next step was to admit his need of others and God to help him find himself and complete himself.

THE WONDERFUL TRUTH

The wonderful truth is that when we awaken to our hearts and turn to One greater than ourselves, we find two things:

1. We are not sufficient.   2. We are valuable.

We make big mistakes, yet we are still wonderfully and uniquely made. We discover that our personal worth comes not from our production or performance, but from our creation.

With that recognition of the heart we begin to see our need to enter into relationship with One who can restore us in our despair, mend our wounds, regenerate our broken hearts, and give us the abundant life to which we are called. We need to ask God to do for us what we cannot do.

The paradox here is that the more we find we cannot do, the more room there is for God to do. In powerlessness lies our strength.

To know God relationally, personally, intimately, is a powerful experience. In the pursuit of an intimate relationship with the Giver of Life, we begin to find our lives reshaped and transformed until we are living in the expression of our hearts' desires. We come to recognize our brokenness, and in our brokenness we find our inheritance of full life.

The paradox here is that the more we find we cannot do, the more room there is for God to do. In powerlessness lies our strength.

By giving it to God we are brought into a personal relationship with God like we have never before experienced. What is *it*? *It* is the truthful exposure of the heart, in all its worth and incapability.

It is our gifts and talents as well as the barriers that keep us from experiencing brokenness and vulnerability and admitting our neediness and limitation.

It is the heart's battle between its created worth, vulnerability, and giftedness, and the pride, toxic shame, anxiety, resentment, apathy, depression, self-pity, and counterfeit fulfillment that keep us from full life.

Giving *it* up allows us to recognize that God has made us with feelings, and now, even as we struggle with doubt, we are still worthwhile—so valuable that God seeks us and calls our names so that we may know our worth and Him.

In the process, we start to understand what it is all about. The walls constructed around our hearts that block truth must come down so that we can live how we are made to live as vulnerable and valuable creatures. Sometimes the beginning of the truth is simply admitting that the walls are there.

The walls constructed around our hearts that block truth must come down so that we can live how we are made to live as vulnerable and valuable creatures.

In realizing our worth, we begin to see what Jesus was talking about when He was asked which commandment was the greatest. He said to love God with all your heart, soul, strength, and mind. He then said that a second "which is like the first" is to love your neighbor as yourself. Jesus said to love yourself. In recognizing the value of yourself, you're recognizing how God made you and others.

Giving From Your Heart

He made you like you are at the roots of your heart. Knowing this allows you to begin to give what you have to your neighbor. The truth is that you cannot love your neighbor unless you love yourself first. If you know the clarity and struggle of your heart, you will give it.

If you have walls around your heart, you will be limited in what you can genuinely offer.

If you are not capable of giving others the truth of your heart, then you will give them lies, even if these lies are well intentioned.

You cannot give what you do not have. If I come over to your house to borrow eggs to finish brownies and you don't have any eggs, I'm not going to get them.

If I come over to your house to borrow your lawnmower to cut my grass, but you don't have one, I'm not going to get one. If you don't have something, no matter how badly either you or I want you to have it, you can't give it.

Likewise, if I come over to your house and need love, and you don't have it, you cannot give it to me.

The only way you can serve others is by having what God made you to have. Through the willingness to surrender to God, you are made fully into who you are.

The two greatest commandments begin to be fulfilled in the recognition of the awakening of the human heart. Unless you're able to recognize the state of your heart, you cannot value mine, and you also cannot hear God's calling.

OPENING THE DOOR

God comes to the door of your heart and knocks. You cannot have life unless you open your heart to God, which means admitting your feelings, needs, desires, longing, and hope.

If, because of our woundedness, we remain closed, then we miss the experience of full living. In our woundedness we don't trust that God's desire is for our gain. We doubt the authenticity of relationships, love, grace, hope, and faith because of past experiences. Previous woundings cause us to intentionally neglect or ignore what is true—that we are created in the image of God for relationship.

However, when we awaken to the value of how we are made, we also awaken to the recognition that others are like us. When we tell the truth about our hearts, ask for help, and reach for God, we will find our hearts moved and enlivened by relationships.

THE GIFT OF FEELINGS

Through feeling your feelings, telling the truth, and giving it to God (the process) in willingness and patience and work and time, you will receive the gifts that are what grown ups experience in life lived fully. Remember, feelings are God's tools that allow us to live fully in a tragic place. Life is tragic and God is faithful. The gifts of feelings allow us to move near our faithful God and in His Presence we cannot help but find our gratitude in the midst of life's risks, loses, and loves. Who would not desire such gifts but those in denial of how they are created?

Truth (Willingness + Patience + Work + Time) = Gift

Willingness. In willingness we allow our hearts to risk hope again in spite of past experiences. Hope and the process allows the emotional and spiritual move beyond the past.

Patience. In patience, we carry the burden of hope by persevering in waiting. Waiting means anticipation without results, and the feelings that come with waiting.

Work. In work, we bring our hearts to what we do with our heads and hands. Work allows us to be "all in" vs. labor—which simply we survive.

Time. In time, we give our hearts to the present and start to take up space in our lives. We become three-dimensional; otherwise, life is measured by the clock ticking more that the life lived.

The Gift of Feelings Chart™

Impairment	Truth (W+P+W+T)=	Gift
Resentment	**HURT**	Healing & Courage
Apathy	**LONELY**	Intimacy
Self-pity	**SAD**	Acceptance
Pride & Depression	**ANGER**	Passion
Anxiety	**FEAR**	Wisdom & Faith
Toxic shame & Contempt	**SHAME**	Humility
Toxic shame & Shamelessness	**GUILT**	Freedom & Forgiveness
Sensuous or sensual pleasure without heart	**GLAD**	Joy with sadness

Powerlessness and vulnerability are about facing that we *can't*, but God *can*. The more powerless and broken we find ourselves, the more room there is for God to move. Ultimately, we have the power to do only one thing—refuse God—which is to refuse how we are made.

All these feelings weave and work together, like the keys on a piano. Touching one doesn't touch the other one, but they're all part of the same. If we learn the great skill of playing them, we can make music that is the heart's symphony of how we're created.

LIVE

No matter where you go with your heart, you will find fuller life because living from your heart awakens your dependency, vulnerability, and neediness for relationship with others and God.

Feel your feelings, tell the truth, and give it to God. The meaning is simple to comprehend, but unless you are willing to turn your heart over to how it was made in vulnerability and brokenness, this simple understanding is impossible to attain.

Feel your feelings—take responsibility for the content of your heart.

Tell the truth—be vulnerable and truthful with others.

Give it to God—ask for help from others and God, and recognize that you are needy and incapable on your own.

Follow life's call—pursue your heart's desires.

Submit to authority—recognize your limitations and listen to words and guidance that helps you grow.

Acknowledge that you matter—there is nothing you can do to be more or less loved by the One who made you.

Recognize what you value—cherish it for what it is, a gift.

Risk loss—you will find joy and success.

Enjoy success—you will find more of God.

Live fully.

Pursue Heart Truths

When I was ten years old, my family had moved out to the country. That is where I met Mrs. J. M. Blair, who at the time was in her sixties. She walked across the road where I was helping my father work on a fence. She brought him a glass of water in a crinkled glass that had imprints of oranges on it. We all visited a while before she returned across the road through an opening in the tall boxwoods that surrounded her place.

The next year I asked Mrs. Blair if I could cut her grass for three dollars, and that is when our relationship began. In the fall, the grass cutting became leaf raking and bush trimming. And when it snowed, I would take coal to her house from her shed, and we would sit in the living room by her furnace.

Mrs. Blair would make apple pies for me in the fall and lemonade with tons of sugar and real lemons in the summer. After school at times, even as I got older, I would visit her and read the newspapers with her on her open back porch while we sat on aluminum fan-chairs. She loved me. I was special to her. I loved her. She was a good person.

Years later after I grew up and was living in Texas, I heard that Mrs. Blair died. I didn't make it back for her funeral. I never told her I loved her. I regret that truth.

I pray that:

You will feel your feelings, tell the truth, and give it to God.

You will let your tears flow and your anger create, but do no harm.

Your loneliness will help you reach for those you need and help you be available to those who need you. Your loneliness will lead you to reach for intimacy with God.

Your sadness will value life, and your hurt bring healing, not death, though there will be scars. Your fear will be the beginning of wisdom.

Through forgiveness and change your guilt will lead you back to humility and freedom.

You will pursue these real heart truths, that your joy will be complete; and, I pray that you will long for more life and deeper truths.

QUESTIONS FOR PERSONAL REFLECTION

1. What are three of your most significant gifts or talents?

2. What are three of your most significant limitations or weaknesses?

3. What walls exist around your heart? How do these wall limit your relationships with others?

4. In what ways is your heart closed to a more intimate relationship with God?

5. What is something for which you deeply hope that is beyond your own power to produce or manipulate into having? What do you feel in desiring so deeply?

6. Do you believe that there is nothing you can do to be more or less loved by the One who made you? How does your answer to this questions affect your relationships with others?

7. What is the greatest area of need in your life (be specific)?

8. Do you believe that through surrender and vulnerability, God can do for you what you cannot do for yourself? What has been your experience with this idea?

CONDITIONS OF THE HEART

The following words describe conditions of the heart and have feeling in them but aren't the feelings themselves.

☞

loved
unimportant
ineffectual
antagonistic
alive
regretful
helpless
vengeful
wanted
bashful
resigned
indignant
lustful
self-conscious
apathetic
hated
worthy
puzzled
shy
unloved
respected
edgy
uncomfortable
friendly

pitied
upset
baffled
regarded
empathetic
reluctant
benevolent
confused
awed
timid
nervous
wide awake
enthusiastic
mixed-up
tempted
at ease
zealous
provoked
relaxed
admired
tense
peaceful
courageous
bitter

liked
detested
worried
sympathetic
comfortable
determined
enchanted
fed up
affectionate
appealing
perplexed
important
contented
stubborn
infatuated
dumb
patient
concerned
troubled
appreciated
daring
pleased
tender
depressed

alarmed	fatigued	forlorn
threatened	amused	kind
disdainful	abandoned	lethargic
eager	provoked	dejected
smart	brave	rejected
interested	consoled	meek
vibrant	intelligent	gloomy
sick	proud	bored
good	peaceful	embarrassed
prayerful	secure	superior
strong	degraded	sexy
optimistic	inspired	bad
shocked	brilliant	inhibited
relieved	cynical	bewildered
independent	wise	discontented
disconsolate	gratified	forlorn
silly	useless	generous
exhausted	popular	center-staged
contemptuous	humiliated	tired
miserable	resentful	disappointed
panicky	unpopular	frightened
venturous	quiet	reflective
capable	suspicious	indifferent
dissatisfied	weak	torn
disgusted	alienated	anxious
impotent	listless	erotic
annoyed	envious	unsure
hopeful	hopeless	inadequate
trapped	virtuous	dismayed
worn out	moody	relieved
great	repulsed	impatient

About the Author
CHIP DODD

☙

Chip Dodd, PhD, is a teacher, trainer, author, and counselor, who has been working in the field of recovery and redemption for over 30 years. It is the territory in which people can return to living the way we are created to live—where we can move from mere survival to living fully, from isolation to loving deeply, and from controlling to leading others well.

In 1996 after receiving his PhD in counseling from the University of North Texas, Chip founded a treatment center in Nashville, TN, where he continues the work of helping patients recover full living.

With his clinical experience, love of storytelling, and passion for living fully, Chip developed a way of seeing and expressing one's internal experience called the Spiritual Root System™. It expresses the essential heart of human beings and gives practical tools to live fully, love deeply, and lead well.

ALSO BY CHIP DODD:

The Perfect Loss: A Different Kind of Happiness
Live Fully: Meditations on Passion
Love Deeply: Meditations on Intimacy
Lead Well: Meditations on Integrity
The Needs of the Heart
Anthem to the Invisible

Find more online at www.sagehillresources.com

About
SAGE HILL

☙

Sage Hill is a social impact organization founded by Chip Dodd, committed to helping others see who they are made to be so they can do what they are made to do.

Wherever life has you, we're here to help you keep heart. We offer recovery and addiction treatment programs, therapeutic counseling, leadership development intensives, corporate consulting, staff retreats, teaching resources, and more. Visit us online for more information.

CPENASHVILLE.COM

The JourneyPure Center for Professional Excellence is a multidisciplinary treatment center for professional men who want to recover their lives, their passions, and their integrity from the effects of addiction, depression, anxiety, and other behavioral problems.

SAGE HILL COUNSELING.COM

When life doesn't work, Sage Hill Counseling is here to help. We offer counseling for individuals, couples, families, children/adolescents, and group therapies to help you heal, grow, and mature. Sage Hill Counseling centers are currently located in Nashville, TN, and Memphis, TN.

SAGE HILL RESOURCES.COM

Sage Hill Resources is dedicated to producing materials that help you keep heart. All of our resources use the wisdom of the Spiritual Root System™ to help you gain a deeper understanding of your heart, which can lead to more authentic relationship with yourself, others, and God.

SAGE HILL TRAINING.COM

Sage Hill Training is a transformational learning experience created to benefit people-helpers from all walks of life to live fully, love deeply and lead well. Specifically designed to profoundly benefit you on both a professional and personal level, this relationship-centered training will help you better serve others with passion, wisdom, and integrity.

Wake up and go home to who you are made to be.

SAGE HILL
A SOCIAL IMPACT ORGANIZATION

The Voice of the Heart

COMPANION BIBLE STUDY

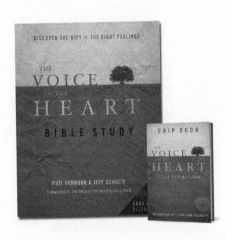

SECOND EDITION
with Companion Bible Study

In 2001, *The Voice of the Heart* began a steady journey into the lives of those looking for more. Since its initial release, *The Voice of the Heart* has been handed one friend to another and has helped thousands of people begin to speak the truth of their story and to live more fully from the heart.

Available online at www.sagehillresources.com

The
PERFECT LOSS

A Different Kind of Happiness

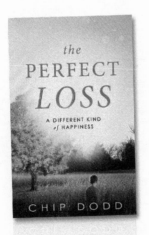

Through the use of story, experience, knowledge, and Scripture, we follow Chip Dodd as he shows us how to walk the path toward a life of passion, intimacy and integrity—leaving a legacy that passes life forward to those we love and beyond.

Though the fig tree does not bud and there are no grapes on the vines, though the olive crop fails and the fields produce no food, though there are no sheep in the pen and no cattle in the stalls, yet I will rejoice in the LORD.

—Habakkuk 3:17-18

Using the Beatitudes, the author shows us the eight movements we all must make if we are to live fully.

Available online at www.sagehillresources.com

LIVE FULLY, LOVE DEEPLY, LEAD WELL

Meditations on Passion, Intimacy, & Integrity

We are created as emotional and spiritual creatures designed to live fully, love deeply, and lead well.

These small books will help you think a little, wonder some, and ponder more. The words can settle into your heart in such a way that you can be reminded of who you are made to be and have more recovery of your life.

Be replenished to live fully each day.

STAY INSPIRED,
KEEP HEART

Connect with Sage Hill

Find daily inspiration, stay current on Sage Hill
events, gain access to free videos, and more.

Subscribe online at www.sagehillresources.com